"Leadership is a precious asset in any c~~~ ~~~ church. This study shows how to recognize and nurture it in ~~~ others. One of the most encouraging books I have read in a long time.
Sr. Doris Gottemoeller, R.S.M.
President, Leadership Conference of Women Religious

"It is not coincidental that while the world suffers a crisis in political, economic, and religious leadership, the literary market is glutted with theories, remedies, and antidotes. The selection of resources is vast, but credible role models are few. Lough Sofield and Don Kuhn fill an important gap. They not only contextualize leadership within the framework of values, but introduce a diverse array of real-life heroes who live out those values daily. *The Collaborative Leader* offers both a theory of Christian leadership and the tools to achieve it —it is inspirational and practical."
Linda Perrone Rooney, D.Min.
Chairperson, National Assn. for Lay Ministry

"Reading this book is like sitting at the feet of some very human but transformative worldly leaders whose Twelve Words of Wisdom challenge all leaders, especially those of us entrusted with 'the care of souls.' A gentle, insightful work, it's the kind of forceful examen of conscience that should confront every present leader and be the measurement for those aspiring. Pastors, parishes, and parish councils would do well to use this marvelous book as an evaluation of their effectiveness."
William J. Bausch, author of *The Total Parish Manual*

"For ages the church has looked to clergy and religious for leadership. But now, in the post-Vatican II period, the laity are emerging as leaders in a wonderful way, not because of title or role as much as in their everyday work and domestic lives. The book clearly and enjoyably explores the ways lay people do this and how their example teaches and inspires us to follow."
Linda D. Amadeo
Executive Editor, *Human Development*

"Not only a contribution to leadership literature, but a must read book for church leaders — and the rest of us."
Ann White, S.L.
Executive Director
National Assn. of Church Personnel Administrators

Br. Loughlan Sofield, S.T., a leading consultant on ministry and personal development, lectures and gives workshops across the United States as well as internationally. He is the author of *Design for Wholeness* and *Collaborative Ministry* (both published by Ave Maria Press), Senior Editor of *Human Development* magazine, and General Councilor of the Missionary Servants of the Most Holy Trinity.

Mr. Donald H. Kuhn, a specialist in leadership development, is active in both business and the church. He recently completed a lengthy career with AT&T where he was Human Resources Director of Employment Development. He is currently Executive Secretary of UNICON, a consortium of major American and European universities which provide executive education. Active within his church community, he serves as a retreat director, workshop leader, and group facilitator.

THE
COLLABORATIVE
LEADER

Listening to the Wisdom
Of God's People

Loughlan Sofield, S.T.
Donald H. Kuhn

Foreword by Dolores Leckey

AVE MARIA PRESS
Notre Dame, Indiana 46556

From Don
to Teeny
Who makes life an exciting collaboration.

and
From Loch
to Carroll, Pete, and Robert
Who have been wisdom people for me.

Some excerpts from THE NEW JERUSALEM BIBLE, copyright© 1985 by Darton, Longman & Todd, Ltd. and Doubleday & Company, Inc. Reprinted by permission of the publisher.

International Standard Book Number: 0-87793-544-0
Library of Congress Catalog Card Number: 94-79357
Printed and bound in the United States of America.

ACKNOWLEDGMENTS

This project was only possible because of the "wisdom people." They are the forty-two people who generously agreed to be interviewed. They graciously and candidly shared their wisdom, insights, and recommendations. Without their contributions, we could not have written this book. We are deeply indebted to them, not only for their responsiveness to our request, but especially for all they have done and continue doing daily to contribute to the growth of the Lord's kingdom.

There are numerous people to whom we will be eternally grateful for their selfless assistance in every stage of the development of the research project and the final manuscript.

First, we are deeply indebted to three people without whose assistance this project would have been virtually impossible: Dawne Fleri for her tireless and painstaking work of typing the selected quotes from each interview; Carroll Juliano, S.H.C.J., for her professional assistance in the final editing of the manuscript; and Marlene Debole for her willingness to provide secretarial service whenever requested.

During the development of the manuscript a number of people agreed to serve as readers and reactors in our attempts to faithfully articulate what we had learned from the interviews. Thank you to each of them; Mary Sofield, Peter Holden, S.T., Rosine Hammett, C.S.C., Juan Lorenzo Hinojosa and Timothy O'Connell.

We are also grateful to the many people who evidenced enough interest in our project to nominate the wisdom people we interviewed. Our appreciation is also extended to David Schlaver, C.S.C., Frank Cunningham, Bob Hamma, and Charles Jones of Ave Maria Press who encouraged us and provided valuable insights as they guided the manuscript through its various drafts.

Finally, it was the generosity of an anonymous foundation which provided us with the financial means to be able to effectively carry out this project.

To each of you we say a profound thank you.

CONTENTS

FOREWORD

Some poignant lines in Psalm 90 speak of human labor in a rather sobering way.

> Seventy is the sum of our years
> or eighty, if we are strong,
> And most of them are fruitless toil
> for they pass quickly, and we drift away.

No doubt countless women and men experience something quite similar to the ancient psalmist. But there are others—the wisdom people they are called in this book—whose work is fruitful in the fullest sense, yielding a harvest of rich meaning. How does it happen that doctors and lawyers, restaurant managers and beauticians, nurses and publishers—people from a variety of occupations—can reach such a deep sense of appreciation that the work they do, day after day year after year, is truly a vocation? A mission, even?

The Collaborative Leader: Listening to the Wisdom of God's People invites us into a conversation with forty-two men and women who responded to the authors' queries about how they view their work, how they apply Christian values to the workplace, what support they receive from the official church, and what they believe lay leaders need from church leaders. As we "listen" to that conversation we learn a great deal about the subjects—what they value in life, who influences their decisions, that they are self-reflective people—and we learn as much about ourselves.

For a strength of this book is that the reader easily enters into the dialogue already underway between the subjects and the authors.

I was intrigued to learn how central fathers had been in the spiritual, religious and values formation of these wisdom people, and I wanted to know more. Why is the church not perceived as a principal agent of formation for them, I wondered? How did Joy (who owns twelve beauty shops) come to fear her divorce alienated her from the church, I asked? Was it something the parish, or certain people, did or did not do? Or was it more of a generalized feeling?

I found myself grateful that the fields of commerce, health, education, law, publishing, cosmetology were blessed with people who struggle to know whether or not they are truly leading lives of integrity. These lay men and women, leaders in their fields, many of them parents of large families, regularly engage in a reflective process to help them see who they are becoming through their professional and family responsibilities and their civic duties, and how they are affecting their environments. One hopes that church leaders are equally humble and serious in their personal examples. For no one is exempt from the psalmist's prayer:

> Teach us to number our days aright
> that we may gain wisdom of heart (Psalm 90).

The Collaborative Leader offers a structure for thoughtful reflection, a necessary step toward the wisdom longed for by the psalmist.

One frequently hears that there is a need to develop a genuinely lay spirituality, i.e., knowing and following Jesus the Christ in the web of the laity's existence: in the family, in the workplace, and in the complexities of modern citizenship. But how can such a spirituality be realized? Jesuit theologian John Coleman suggests that what is needed is a "new kind of talking," meaning small groups of women and men who together do what the subjects of *The Collaborative Leader* did with authors Sofield and Kuhn: speak about the influence of God's Holy Spirit in their everyday lives. The subjects made an interesting discovery, namely that the interviews themselves became another means of spiritual formation as they sought to articulate the deepest parts of their life experience; and out of these depths came a certain kind of wisdom.

As small groups of Christians gather for prayer and study, *The Collaborative Leader* can be a useful resource for getting in touch with the meaning of their own work and with the power of their unique vocations. In my imagination I see small communities of young people—teachers, nurses, business managers, librarians, editors, computer specialists—married and single, regularly meeting to explore how they are following Christ in their professions, how they are failing, what changes they need to make. I see older people, too, the seasoned leaders in their fields, measuring the reality of their work against the ideal. I see retired persons who still "work," although not for pay, using their perfected expertise to care for some segment of human need. I see all of these "workers in the vineyard" moving from talk to prayer, perhaps to the petition in Psalm 90:

> Prosper the work of our hands for us,
> prosper the work of our hands!

I see what is possible. And I feel hopeful once again that despite the rampant cynicism and divisiveness (often in religious guise) which are stifling our societal soul, there are still people of integrity and compassion who quietly go about the work of Christ. These are the blessed: the peacemakers, the merciful, those hungry for righteousness and justice. These are the wisdom people; may their number increase.

> Dolores R. Leckey
> Executive Director
> Secretariat for Family, Laity, Women and Youth

Introduction

This is a book about Christian leadership. It offers a blueprint drawn from the recommendations and lives of forty-two Christians whom we call the "wisdom people." Committed to living out their values in the workplace, these are people who carry Christ's message to those they encounter in their daily lives. They lead organizations, run beauty parlors, provide meals in local restaurants, build houses in suburban towns, and sit in busy Washington offices working on public policy. These are leaders whose credibility to speak of Christian leadership emerges from who they are, what they do, and most importantly how they make decisions and impact the world around them.

As we explored the idea of taking a fresh look at Christian leadership, we were influenced by the words of Pope Paul VI in his encyclical *Evangelization in the Modern World*:

Above all the gospel must be proclaimed by witness.... Through this wordless witness these Christians stir up irresistible questions in the hearts of those who see how they live: Why are they like this? Why do they live in this way? What or who inspires them? Why are they in our midst?

His concept of "wordless witness" provided a key for our focus. Through his questions he pointed to the areas that we might explore. As we started our work, we quickly became convinced that what can be learned from these witnesses can help the church to be more effective in carrying out its divine mission.

The concept of leadership which we present in these pages emerges from a series of interviews in which we pursued the ques-

11

tions raised by Paul VI. Our journey began with searching out people from all walks of life so we might tap into their wisdom and experience, gleaning insights which could be helpful to those in church leadership.[1] We wanted to fathom responses to such questions as: How do leaders have to change? What should they make their priorities? Where should they concentrate their energies? Are they adequately responding to the needs of people?

In addition to hearing their answers to these questions, we also wanted to learn about the lives of these people and the daily challenges they face as they witness to their Christian values in the workplace. We wanted to know them both as individuals and as committed Christians who have expectations of the church. From an analysis of the considerable body of information we collected, we wanted to formulate a model of Christian leadership and offer recommendations for change.

Church leaders, as we define them, are all those in positions to effect the development of members of the Christian community. This includes hierarchy, lay leaders, ordained ministers, members of religious congregations, educators and administrators of church-related programs, parish and diocesan staff members, pastoral council members, spiritual directors, and those in retreat ministry or lay ministry formation programs. As you will see, we believe that leadership is the dominant force within a church organization. How individuals in authority carry out their roles has profound impact on people both within and outside the church.

This was certainly true for those we interviewed. They did not always speak of a leader in terms of a single individual at the top of a group. They talked about people with varied levels of responsibility for setting direction, moving things forward, and rallying others together. While each interview was unique, the more we spoke with people, the more common themes and characteristics emerged. What we heard contributed to a clear definition of what is required of Christian leaders. We heard about the source and formation of people's values and about conflicts between their values and those held by the larger society. We heard pleas for understanding and support and for help when things get difficult. We heard of their relationship to the church as an institution which overemphasizes ministry within the institution, often overlooking the fact that the principal ministry of most people is carrying Christian values to the world. We heard complaints from thoughtful and mature people who sense that the church steps back from the messy questions of the day-to-day, taking a more compartmentalized view of life that creates a gulf between their faith and the Monday-to-Friday realities of their work lives.

The way in which the wisdom people spoke of these issues revealed them as passionate people. They have a deep love of God and have high expectations of the church. They are not bitter, cynical, or negative. For the most part, they are active church members who are nourished by the sacramental life of the church, who understand the church's value to the larger society, who appreciate the church's charitable outreach, and who turn to the church for the experience of community. But they want to see the institution strengthened; they want to see it refocus on what is most important; they worry that it is not living up to its potential and that it may be growing irrelevant. They hope that their insights will help to influence leaders to make the church all it can be.

Today, our bookstores are filled with discussions of leadership from the reflections of Plato to the latest theories on corporate management. Ours is not a traditional book in that vein. Our primary theme is that leadership for Christians is a subtle but powerful quality that is transformative, that brings God's kingdom to reality.

Our purpose, therefore, is twofold. First, we want to talk to leaders in the church to let them hear, with a minimum of filtering, the expectations of people they aspire to lead. We believe it important that they understand the attitudes, needs, and strengths of women and men who are attempting to transform the world. We will present anecdotes, quotations from the interviews, and summary observations about these remarkable people. We will make recommendations as to how leaders in formal ministry might examine themselves and change to meet the challenges, expectations, and needs of their members.

The cumulative impact of the comments made by the wisdom people should not lead the reader to conclude that there are not effective Christian leaders. There are many, and the wisdom people cite their experience with those who exemplify the kinds of behaviors they believe are needed within the church. We are presenting a broad view of leadership, identifying its critical components so that today's leaders, both new and experienced, can reflectively shape their approach to ministry. We hope that the criticisms leveled by the wisdom people will not cause defensiveness or guilt on the part of the reader. We believe that providing tools for self-examination by both individuals and groups will foster enhanced leadership in the church.

While our primary emphasis is on the need for leadership change and development, we recognize that any change involving leaders also involves change and development for the organizations and people they lead. We suggest, therefore, that the concepts and recommendations which are framed for leaders also be used by groups to examine their expectations of both their leaders and themselves. Change and growth within any organization are an organic process involving all its parts. All flourish or wither in relationship to each other.

Secondly, we want to talk to laity to affirm their responsibility for leadership in the world. We want to encourage all Christians to respond more completely to their baptismal call, to take risks, and to put their values on the line. We believe that some people have a limited sense of their own power and that they somehow think that it is only "the others" who can bring about change. Our hope is to counter that mindset by telling the stories of people who, in widely-varied occupations, eagerly accept and use the power available to them to force change, make a difference, and minister as Christ did.

We are also concerned about the many people we meet who are either unaware of their vocation in the world or are aware of it but feel isolated, alone, and unsupported by the church. We hope that the stories of people who have clarity about their vocation will speak to them and reveal how one's occupation and one's spiritual life can be integrated. When presenting our findings in workshops, we have seen the excitement of people who gain clarity about their own call to Christian vocation as a result of listening to these stories.

In writing this book, we grappled with an impossible task: how can we communicate accurately what we heard? The accuracy is not so much in being faithful to *what* was said. We believe we have done that to the best of our ability. What is impossible to convey is the emotion generated in us by each of the interviews. We would return from them excited, exhilarated, personally challenged, and filled with hope. The energy which the wisdom people generate confirms the message of Jesus: "I have come so that they may have life and have it to the full" (John 10:10). These people are the flesh and blood reality of that statement.

The wisdom people whom we quote are people of integrity and action. They are not plaster saints. They are not always successful. They are sometimes troubled by crises of faith. They are not insulated from pain and suffering. But they are transformative. They have learned how to take life experience and integrate it into their value and decision-making processes. They are reflective people who know what they believe and why. They are exciting people who, in Jesus' words, are hot or cold, never lukewarm.

The first chapter presents a composite view of the wisdom people. The second delineates a leadership model based on the recommendations of the wisdom people. Chapters three through ten develop those recommendations which relate to the role of leaders. The final four chapters focus on the person of the leader. Effective leadership is more than doing things. It involves the more difficult aspect of personal transformation.

We welcome you to this exploration, hoping that it will be stimulating and challenging, open opportunities for self-discovery, and move you to personal growth and action both in your own life and in the lives of those you touch through your ministry.

Most importantly, we raise the question: Do we truly believe as Christians we *can* transform the world? Are we convinced faith is a force for change? Recall the story from Matthew which tells of Jesus walking on the water toward the boat holding his disciples. Anxious to go out and greet him, Peter asks for help, but once out on the water, starts sinking. And Jesus sadly exclaims, "You have so little faith. Why did you doubt?" (Matthew 14:31).

The Wisdom People: Biographical Data

Throughout this book you will encounter the forty-two wisdom people we were privileged to interview. Through their recommendations and lives they provided the data on which this model of Christian leadership has been developed. These short "biographies" are meant to give you some background on each of the people you will discover in the ensuing pages. Each of them was asked to identify her/himself by a name.

Angel was born to Mexican American parents in 1930. His family had fled from Mexico during the revolution. Angel's entire professional career has been in the field of education. Twenty years ago he founded an educational research and advocacy organization which focuses on the needs of minority children. He has felt himself alienated from the Catholic church because he perceives a lack of commitment to the poor and minorities.

Anthony is a medical doctor, an internist. He attempts to be "pastoral" with his patients. His primary values are "listening to and helping the patients respond to their needs." He is married and the father of nine children.

Arthur holds a chair in the College of Business Administration at a midwestern university. He has been chosen as "the outstanding teacher" by the students on more than one occasion. He specializes in research on multinational corporations, exploring the relationship of profit and poverty in developing nations. Arthur is sixty-one years of age.

Caroline is fifty-seven years of age. She describes herself as having two vocations being single and being a Catholic educator. She is principal of an elementary school which has operated for approximately twenty-five years without assigned religious sisters. She strongly believes that building a faith community is a basic, differentiating feature of a parochial institution.

Chris is an executive who has been in the publishing business for thirty years. He is fifty-two years of age, married and the father of four grown children. While he continues to be a faithful churchgoer, Chris is frustrated by the fact that churches have become "largely irrelevant."

Colman is fifty-four years of age, married with three sons. He is a syndicated columnist for a large urban newspaper. With his wife he has established the Center for Teaching Peace. He lectures and teaches at high schools, colleges, and universities.

David, age sixty-eight, is a senior partner in a major law firm which serves corporate clients in a large eastern city. He is married and is the father of seven children. He serves on many religious, educational, and civic boards, a number of which operate on a national level.

Dawne is a wife, mother and administrative assistant. She is fifty-three years old and has been married for thirty-five years. The marriage has produced ten children, seven of whom are still living and are in their twenties and early thirties. Dawne is a convert to Catholicism. One of her dreams is that the church will be a place where people come to share their story.

Elizabeth is a registered nurse involved in enterostomal therapy, a specialty she entered nineteen years ago when her father had a temporary colostomy. She is the member of a team of nurses who stress complete concern for the patients in their care (those with wounds, ostomies, and continence needs). Their focus is on rehabilitation/comfort. Elizabeth is fifty-seven years old and single.

Frat is a physician. He had planned to go to Southeast Asia to serve as a medical missionary for the suffering people in that area. He then realized that he was surrounded by poor people who needed him and his skills at the county hospital where he was then serving. Frat has a strong desire to share what he has with others. He places great emphasis on the development of his medical team.

Gretchen is a fifty-two year old mother and grandmother. She is also the executive director of an educational service center, providing assistance to 173 schools, with students speaking seventy-four different languages. She is the daughter of Canadian immigrants, who were socialists and avowed agnostics.

Eugene is fifty-seven years old. He is president of a publishing company. He moved often as a child and had been in twelve different schools by the time he was in the eighth grade. He describes himself as "blowing hot and cold on religion from embracing religion with all my heart and energy to rejecting all organized religion and embracing atheism." He is married to Gretchen and they are members of a dynamic parish.

Francis was the second youngest male we interviewed. He is thirty-seven years of age and engaged. He is employed as a software development director with a large computer software company. Francis has a dual commitment to "service" and "balanced living."

George is a builder who started his career working for the government. Convinced that he would not find fulfillment within the bureaucracy, he took the risk of setting up his own construction company. He is married and the father of three. Despite his financial success, he lives simply in the house he bought early in his career.

Grace is forty-nine years of age, married, and the mother of five boys between the ages of eleven and nineteen. Born in Belize, she is now manager of financial planning in a hospital accounting department. Her non-work activities involve her in community organizing at both the local and national level. She networks with others to address justice and peace issues in her diocese and sees her role at work as "reflecting God's love and his preferential option for the poor."

Hillman is an African-American, raised in the South. He is a lawyer and is currently a member of the state House of Representatives. Deeply committed to his work, Hillman lives with the conviction that "there is life after death and life after politics." His primary legislative concerns are quality education and adequate, affordable housing for all. He is married and the "proud father" of two children. Hillman's father is a Baptist minister.

Irene with her husband, Randy, is the owner of two restaurants. She is fifty-three years of age. She is a convert to Catholicism. For her the restaurants are more than just businesses. They are an opportunity to create a family ambience for both the customers and the staff. She identified her basic values as "caring, concern, and compassion."

Randy, the husband of Irene, in addition to owning and running the two restaurants, is chairman of a bank. He has been working since he was a young boy and got into the restaurant business as a result of helping his father with the business. He and his wife share identical values.

Jack is sixty-five years of age, married with five children in their thirties. He is a television and movie director and producer, and recently was the recipient of a prestigious entertainment industry award. He is a "recovering alcoholic", who has just had his "fourteenth birthday," something he cherishes as "a gift."

Kate is a television scriptwriter and the wife of Jack. With her husband, she is very involved in programs which foster media literacy. She serves on a committee which attempts to develop a bridge between the media industry and the church hierarchy. She is involved in a number of programs responding to the needs of the less fortunate.

Jim married at age eighteen and has been married for over twenty-six years. He is forty-four years of age and the father of four children. Jim has experienced a series of personal, professional and financial "setbacks" which have strengthened his faith. He is now vice president and part-owner of a construction firm, and plays a leadership role in several construction, community, and church related organizations. Through these organizations, Jim and his wife serve the community. They are involved in ministering to the needs of the homeless and disadvantaged.

Joe is sixty-two years of age, married, and the father of two children. He is the president and CEO of a multimillion dollar company with over six hundred employees. He attempts to know each of his employees and strives to build a climate of family among the employees. He serves as a member of the board of a food bank.

John is an attorney, the senior partner in a firm which he joined early in his career and which has grown to be one of the largest in the state. His principal work is handling the defense in civil cases. Married and the father of three sons, John is in his mid-fifties. His Episcopal parish is an important part of his life.

Joy was "born and raised a Catholic," but feels alienated from her church because of the church's attitude about her divorce. She was originally a nurse but decided to go into hairdressing. She now owns twelve beauty shops and schools with about 150 employees.

In her business she tries to communicate compassion and sensitivity to her employees and clients.

Kaylujan is a widow, about sixty years of age, and a very lively member of a state legislature. Blessed with energy and good humor, she has long been active in local and state politics in addition to serving on local hospital and community boards. She attributes her success to the training she had in raising four sons. She finds great support in her Presbyterian congregation.

Kevin is forty-two years of age, married and the father of three sons. He had his own carpet installation business but is now employed as a sales representative for a trucking/freight company. He describes himself as "a stepping stone," influencing others to deepen their own relationship with the Lord. He is strongly committed to his charismatic prayer group.

Lee describes herself as a "mother and hairdresser." She is forty years of age, married, and the mother of three boys ages twenty to twenty-two and one daughter, age four. While Lee attends church every week, she doesn't feel any kind of "special connection" with the church.

Marge is thirty-eight years of age, single, and a speech pathologist in an elementary school. Her desire is to be empathic as Jesus was empathic. She discovers that her encounter with "hurting people" is what "pulls" that response from her. She has learned that when "you open yourself to their pain, it becomes your pain."

Mark is sixty years of age, married, and the father of three children, all in their thirties. He has been in an executive position in a number of businesses. In 1983 he retired, but the retirement lasted only "seventy-two hours." He is chairman and CEO of a company which employs over sixteen hundred full-time employees and another seven hundred seasonal employees. He has had the opportunity to write and lecture about the role of the Christian in business.

Mimi is a "happily-married" travel agent. She is thirty-two years of age, the youngest woman we interviewed. She places a high value on family life and, as a result, is committed to making life more comfortable for her customers who must spend long periods of time away from their families.

Mirta is a native Cuban who fled to the United States with her two small children over thirty years ago. One of the most profound faith experiences for Mirta has been facing her daughter's cancer. It forced her to the realization that "you have nothing except God and God is *never more present* than in pain and suffering. The way of the cross is the only one leading to resurrection." Mirta recently retired as a school administrator.

Nancy is single, forty-one years of age and a lawyer employed by the United States Congress. Nancy finds a great deal of excitement in being involved in the legislative process. She comes from a long line of attorneys. Both her father and grandfather were also lawyers.

Pat is employed by a professional athletic team as the nutrition coach. She also lectures on health-related issues. Pat is forty-nine years of age, divorced, and currently single. She served two tours of duty in Viet Nam as a triage nurse and has worked in the nursing and health-related fields all her life. She formerly was a university professor.

Paul is an organization change consultant who has worked with social and economic development projects in Third World countries. He also does diversity consulting with American corporations and communities. His interest in bridging cultural gaps is, in part, the result of his father's work with an airline which provided frequent travel during Paul's youth. In his thirties, Paul is completing doctoral studies and intends to continue his work through consulting, research, and teaching.

Peter married right out of college. He is fifty-five years of age. He was originally involved in marketing and advertising. He recently sold his real estate business and is now self-employed in development and real estate projects. Peter is involved in the leadership of a nonprofit group which provides affordable housing for low income families. Since the 1960s he has been very involved in working for politicians and political and social causes.

Raymond is an African-American police officer, who grew up in "a real poverty area" in south Florida. He is thirty-one years of age and engaged to be married. He has been the recipient of numerous awards for the initiatives he has undertaken on behalf of poor, young people in his area.

Richard is the second eldest of the twelve children his mother had. His parents were divorced when he was four years of age, and Richard grew up on welfare, living in projects. He is married and the father of two. He has had a number of different jobs, initially working as a policeman, a human resources specialist for a major corporation, and is currently employed by a consulting firm as a management consultant.

Robert is "a native Southerner." He is an attorney with a civil law practice. He began practicing with his firm in 1970. Through this entire period, he has remained a member of the same parish. Robert is fifty-two years old, married, and the father of two young-adult daughters. He is the youngest of twelve children.

Scott is a union organizer who has been especially effective with immigrant workers from Mexico and Central America. He worked with Caesar Chavez and the United Farm Workers for a number of years, an experience which had a profound influence on him. It was there he realized that people with strong faith convictions are "very special people." Scott is forty-three years of age, married, and the father of six children ranging in age from two to nineteen.

Sharon is forty-one years of age, single, and employed as a vice-president of human resources. She takes an "aggressive approach" in hiring the disabled from various local supportive employment agencies. She particularly sees her role as creating a work environment that is respectful and compassionate toward all individuals. Sharon believes that people in her organization would describe her as "working for their betterment." Formerly she was employed as a director of liturgy in a parish.

Ted operates a large quality assurance organization for a major manufacturer. His work has kept him in the same geographic area where he was born. Though he now lives in the suburbs, he maintains periodic contact with his original innercity church. He is married and the father of three daughters.

Tom was a senior middle-level manager with a major utility company before his retirement. He is married and the father of six grown children. Originally a Midwesterner, he was introduced to the West Coast through service in the Marines. He has spent his adult years there. He is athletic and runs competitively. Currently working with the poor and homeless, he also coaches business people to become more effective in their work relationships.

Notes

[1] For a fuller description of the process and methodology of the interview, see appendices A, B, and C.

I
THE ESSENCE OF
LEADERSHIP:

Jesus and
The Wisdom People

1
The Wisdom People: Models for Christian Leaders

Modern man listens more willingly to witnesses than to
teachers, and if he does listen to teachers, it is because
they are witnesses.

Paul VI

At a recent meeting, a panel of academics and theorists debated
a proposed agenda for the church of the future. About an hour into
the program we experienced *deja vu*: we had heard or read similar
recommendations from these and other experts many times in the
past. People had listened, had taken ideas back to their congregations, and had tried to implement them. Yet it seemed that little
changed. Perhaps, we speculated, the problem lay with the im-
plementation, people simply did not follow through with the plans
they laid out. Or perhaps the recommendations themselves were
flawed, built on a set of assumptions which did not match the
experience of the congregations they were intended to help. Or could
it be that the wisdom everyone sought might reside in an entirely
different, as yet untapped, group of people. If the Spirit is present
within the community, we reflected, maybe we have to listen to
different voices. Because of our interest in exploring aspects of
leadership, we decided to turn to those people of God who, responding to their vocation in the workplace, attempt to live day-to-day
what they understand to be the essence of a Christian life.

Thus began the journey to identify the wisdom people, to hear
the Spirit speaking through them, and to learn what they might say
so that we could develop new paradigms for Christian leadership.

This journey is the process described in the Introduction and in the Appendices.

The Wisdom People

In this chapter we introduce you to forty-two people. They became known to us through their peers who identified them as truly living their Christian values and vocation in the workplace and influencing those they encounter. We spent many hours talking with these people, listening to their words, and to the meanings and feelings beneath those words. We wanted to glean all we could and develop a corporate sense of the wisdom they possess. What we heard from them was not only their own dreams, visions, and hopes, but those of vast numbers of Christians who live their values and vocations daily in the workplace. After analyzing what we heard in the interviews, we formulated the recommendations for effective Christian leadership offered in chapter two.

We characterize these people as *wisdom people* because they speak with wisdom born of a deep relationship with God and nurtured by experience, integrity, and faithfulness. We know that they would be adverse to describing themselves this way, being much more comfortable with the label of "ordinary Christians." While they are painfully aware of their frailties, weaknesses, and faults, their peers see them as outstanding Christians, witnessing to their essential values by the way they live their lives in the workplace.

They are, first and foremost, holy people whose holiness is revealed through their commitment to justice and compassion.

These are not holier-than-thou, ethereal people. These are people you may encounter daily in the office or grocery store; people with whom you socialize; people who laugh and cry with you, fight with you, annoy you, and challenge you. But, primarily, they edify you. They are as diverse as the Christian community women and men, single and married, people from a variety of ethnic and racial backgrounds, old and young, living in many parts of the United States, having broad theological diversity, and spanning a wide range of occupations. Their common denominator is that they were singled out by their peers for their Christian values.

Profile of the Interviewees
- 16 women and 26 men
- ranging in age from 30 to 66

- 6 people in their 30s, 11 in their 40s, 16 in their 50s and 9 in their 60s
- 31 Catholics and 11 Episcopalians, Presbyterians, members of the Church of Christ, and Baptists
- 36 Caucasians, 3 Afro-Americans, and 3 Hispanic Americans
- living in 16 different states and the District of Columbia
- working as beauticians, executives, law enforcement personnel, managers, entrepreneurs, nurses, doctors, lawyers, consultants, teachers, legislators, and other professions
- 33 are married and 9 currently single
- 3 couples where both wife and husband were interviewed

A Description of the Wisdom People

The most striking aspect of the people we interviewed is that they, as individuals and as a group, are among the most alive, self-actualized, generative people we have encountered. Though they are far from perfect, they appear to be relatively comfortable with their imperfections and accept their own flawed humanity .

The wisdom people have two dominant characteristics. First, they are people of intense integrity who feel compelled to do the right thing, the fair thing, the just thing. While this is true of many people, they also have the courage necessary to pursue integrity regardless of its personal consequences. Second, they are generative people who are motivated by a concern for others. Their focus is to discover ways in which their personal lives and actions implicitly and explicitly impact the people around them. They recognize their own power to influence and bring positive change to the broader social context in which they live. The marriage of their personal integrity and their generativity drives their concern for the welfare of others. Their motivation is not a vague humanism, a naive sense of "doing good," or a moral sense of obligation. It is rooted in their deep religious faith and their personal spirituality.

In addition to having integrity and generativity as major values, the wisdom people can also be described in other ways:

They are people of compassion. While they may use a variety of terms, they speak mostly about compassion as a dominant motivational force in their lives. They do not merely talk about compassion; they *act* compassionately as their stories will reveal.

They are highly reflective people. They have developed a capacity for dealing with the traumatic, negative, and often devastating experiences of life without moving to bitterness and cynicism. Many talked of major traumas in their lives: life-threatening illnesses, sudden deaths, and personal injustice. They often discover God's will and his gifts to them in the midst of personal tragedy. Many thanked us for the interview because it provided an occasion for further reflection, challenged them to new insights, and stretched them in terms of self-understanding and self-honesty. Verbalizing their most deeply felt experiences was seen as another growth experience.

As a result of their capacity for reflection, they are people who have developed an advanced degree of self-knowledge and appear relatively comfortable identifying and describing their strong and weak points.

While generally comfortable with the self they discover, they are also very critical of themselves because they do not measure up to the extremely high ego ideals and self-expectations they set for themselves. They are clearly "works in progress."

They are simple, humble people with their humility sometimes tending toward self-deprecation. They apologetically compare themselves with others whom they see as true Christian witnesses. Some could not fathom why anyone would nominate them for a project such as ours.

They are people whose acceptance of simplicity as a fundamental viewpoint often extends to their lifestyle choices. Although many of the people we interviewed had the financial means to live a more comfortable and self-indulgent lifestyle, a significant number intentionally chose to live modestly, depriving themselves of things which many of their contemporaries would consider necessities. In this, as in other of their views, they are counter-cultural. They stress values which run contrary to those prevailing in our society, especially consumerism and materialism. A number of them had opportunities to move to positions with greater financial rewards, but declined based on their conviction that they were where God wanted them to be and where they could do the most good for others.

In spite of their counter-cultural stance which puts them in conflict with others, most of the wisdom people do not experience a significant level of stress. While their values prompt them to make decisions which can have serious financial, career, and personal implications, they experience serenity and peace in their lives. This was very evident during the interviews; they were comfortable people to be with. Their strong Christian-value system, their willingness to make difficult ethical and moral decisions, and their underlying peacefulness reveal a persona attractive to those they encounter. A number of them reported that others in their work environment seek them out to discuss situations where values are involved.

They enjoy a sense of integration and balance in their lives, albeit a precarious one. They are not people who believe that they "have it all together." Rather, like each of us they struggle with the daily choices they must make to achieve and maintain equilibrium in their lives.

Values of the Wisdom People

They are people of deep faith, hungering for a deeper relationship with God. This is a universal phenomenon among them, although the way that faith is nurtured and expressed is diverse. For most, their faith has developed through some form of relationship or community rather than in isolation.

In general, they relate positively to ministry as an appropriate way to describe what they were doing in the marketplace. Whether familiar or not with the term "ministry," they have a sense of Christian vocation which enriches what they do and how they do it. Their integrity prompts them to infuse their work with a meaning and significance larger than the mere accomplishment of tasks. In this way, they are people who broaden the concept of ministry beyond that understood by many people.

In addition to our being able to identify the characteristics of the wisdom people from our research, we learned a great deal which we will describe in the pages to follow. Some general observations, however, are of special interest.

The greatest diversity among the wisdom people is in their relationship with and evaluation of the church. They span a spectrum from painful alienation to casual membership, from extreme ambivalence to steadfast commitment. For some, the church is their source of consolation and support. For others, it is a major disappointment, failing to live up to their ideal of what constitutes a Christian church, from both a hierarchical and communal standpoint.

The major influences on the development of their values has been the family, with surprising emphasis on the role of the father. Linking back to what we spoke about earlier, it is clear that self-reflection and integration of life experience has had significant impact on values development.

Their support comes from a variety of sources. Most talked about the importance of close friends and of people they know professionally. Quite consistently, men spoke of their wives as the people who filled the friend-support role. Interestingly, most of the married women did not position their husbands in that way. Few spoke of turning to church leaders to fill a support role.

The interviewees, while at first reluctant to believe that they could offer anything of significance to church leaders, came to a realization that they had much to offer. As they talked with us, it became obvious to them that they were speaking of things which are important to them and about which, sadly, no one had asked them before. They want the church to be so much more than it is, but they feel that leadership is not especially interested in their viewpoints.

The summary of characteristics possessed by the wisdom people and our additional findings raise a number of critical questions which might be valuable for personal self-reflection by church leaders:

- Do these people model for me the person and leader I want to be?
- In what ways do I want or need to change so that I can be a more effective leader?
- What does the description of the wisdom people tell me about many of the people whom I lead?
- What does reflection on the qualities of the wisdom people say to me about forming and influencing those in the Christian community I am called to serve?
- How can I determine whether I possess the characteristics which the wisdom people have?

Finally, there are the overriding pastoral questions:

- How can I serve these people's needs as they face the challenges of their lives?
- How can I create a Christian community which develops exemplar Christians such as these?

These last two questions are interrelated. Edwin Friedman, a rabbi and family systems specialist who works with business and religious systems, states:

> The key to successful leadership has more to do with the leader's capacity for self-definition than with ability to motivate others . . . . Ultimately, it is less a matter of how the "coach" manages his players and more a matter of how he manages himself.

If, as Friedman suggests, self-transformation is the more important ingredient for effective leadership, the characteristics of the wisdom people serve as a useful model for self-evaluation.

We are convinced that the forty-two Christians whom we have introduced are those who speak with different voices that must be listened to; we believe they are representative of the rich resources which exist in the church community but are ignored. By listening to the insights and tapping into the wisdom of these people and others like them, we will be much more in touch with the call and will of the Spirit. Their primary criteria for making decisions can be captured with three questions:

- What is the right thing to do in these circumstances?
- How can I have the most positive impact on others?
- What guidance does Jesus give to help in making the correct choice?

Hearing how the wisdom people reflect on and respond to these questions should be of vital interest to church leaders. Studying their lives, their struggles, their attitudes, their convictions, and their recommendations will help Christian ministers deepen their knowledge of ways to effectively "equip the saints for the work of the kingdom." Their knowledge and expectations challenge all in leadership roles with new ways to understand and perform ministry.

Having introduced the wisdom people, we will present, in chapter two, a distillation of their wisdom as it pertains to effective Christian leadership.

Reflection Questions

In addition to the reflection questions incorporated in this chapter, the following may be helpful for both individuals and groups. While written in the first person singular, the questions below and at the end of all the chapters can be restated in the plural for groups wanting to analyze leadership within their communities.

1. Who are the wisdom people whom I have encountered, people who attempt to live their Christian values to the fullest?

2. Am I willing to search them out and tap into their wisdom?

2
Christian Leadership:
The Key Elements

> This Jesus who has been taken up from you into heaven
> will come back in the same way as you have seen.
>
> Acts 1:11

Jesus is the indispensable model for Christian leaders. What is revealed in his teachings and his life speaks to all believers who serve as leaders; it shapes the way in which they understand their roles and act as people who can transform the world. In him they see the focus, characteristics, and behavior that are needed to build God's kingdom.

For church leaders, the Jesus model is even more compelling because it is through the church that the message of God's love and abiding presence is revealed to the larger community. Profoundly shaped and influenced by its leaders, the institution itself is a testament to the validity of the gospel message. If the workings of the church do not reveal that message, where can people experience it?

What differentiates Jesus as a leader is his all-abiding and foundational belief in God's love. His constant message is that God's love is transforming, provided we respond in three ways: by loving God as the source of life and hope, by loving ourselves as an expression of God's personal and free gift to us, and by loving others as revelations of God and his goodness. Throughout his life, Jesus taught the message of love, his words and actions constantly reinforcing each other. His final charge to his followers was that they go out to the whole world to reveal the good news. Regarding those who believe, he said:

> These are the signs that will be associated with believers:
> in my name they will cast out devils; they will have the

> gift of tongues; they will pick up snakes in their hands
> and be unharmed should they drink deadly poison; they
> will lay their hands on the sick, who will recover (Mark
> 16:17-18).

These are strong words. They dramatically emphasize the power of belief in God's love as transforming. The seemingly impossible can be realized.

The critical role of the church is its responsibility to carry on Jesus' mission, to promulgate the reality of divine love, and to manifest its active and ongoing presence in the world. A primary concern of both the church and its leaders, therefore, is helping all people experience that love and achieve a deeper communion with their God. As that happens, they are moved to personal acts of love, reflecting the model which Jesus revealed.

How did Jesus express his love? The scriptures are filled with his teachings, with the stories he told, and with incidents in which he showed how words are translated into action. While the gospel speaks to everyone and is the guide for all believers, it carries special meaning for those in leadership roles who are called to carry Jesus' message to the modern world.

Jesus as the Model for Christian Leadership

The leadership model which can be drawn from the teachings and life of Jesus is a rich source for personal reflection and inspiration. While each leader is unique and carries out his or her responsibilities in ways that reflect personality, training, and culture, the basic characteristics and behaviors which are revealed in the Jesus model are applicable to all.

Jesus was a listener, patiently attending to people's stories, hearing the pain, the hopes, and the joy of life. When Jesus visits Martha and Mary, he deals compassionately with an event as ordinary as a domestic rivalry, giving a surprising answer to Martha's complaint. He does not change the situation, but clearly hears and responds to her (Luke 10:38-42).

Jesus was responsive in a loving way to what he heard. There is the story, for example, of the request from Jairus that Jesus heal his daughter. While on the way to the house, Jesus is distracted by the woman who, suffering from hemorrhage, touches his cloak with the result that by the time he reaches Jairus' house, the child has died. Jesus calmly enters, says that she is sleeping and commands her to get up. The final human touch in the story is that Jesus says with simple directness, "Give her something to eat" (Mark 5:21-43).

Jesus was a creator of vision, holding up a view of the future and indicating a direction for getting there, but not prescribing detailed steps to be followed. The beatitudes are such a vision. They speak to a new world where pain and suffering are acknowledged and integrated into people's lives as a means of achieving wholeness and union with God (Matthew 5:1-12).

Jesus was authentic, letting himself be known for who he was. He was not reluctant to share his fears with the apostles and to ask for their support. Mark reports (14:34) that as Jesus went into the garden with them to pray, "Distress and anguish came over him, and he said to them, 'The sorrow in my heart is so great that it almost crushes me. Stay here and watch.'" Having admitted his vulnerability, he prays, only to learn that their support is not forthcoming. They fall to sleep.

Jesus was compassionate, being with people, sharing their feelings, and responding to their pain. The gospels are replete with examples of Jesus' compassion. His whole life was characterized by compassionate responses to those who experience pain of mind, body, or soul. Matthew sums up the ministry of Jesus, recounting a series of miracles and declaring that "And when he saw the crowds he had compassion for them" (Matthew 9:36).

Jesus was forgiving, freely taking away people's burdens and helping them set a new direction in their lives. His sensitivity to the woman taken in adultery makes that encounter all the more powerful. He forces her accusers away with a single question about their own guilt. Only then does he deal directly with the woman, urging her to sin no more (John 8:1-11).

Jesus was straightforward, being direct and not dependent on rules and procedures to solve problems. One of his many interactions with the Pharisees involved their questioning him about his disciples' gathering wheat on the Sabbath. Typical of these exchanges, he moves away from the intricacies of the law to deal with the meaning: "The Sabbath was made for man; not man for the Sabbath" (Mark 2:23-28).

Jesus was generative, continually focused on others rather than on self. Such behavior started at the very beginning of his ministry with the miracle at the Cana marriage feast. (John 2:1-11) That pattern is repeated over and over as Jesus responds to request after request for help.

Jesus was inclusive, wanting all to enter into the fullness of life. Matthew's gospel closes with Jesus charging his disciples: "Go, therefore, make disciples of all nations" (Matthew 28: 19).

Jesus was empowering, giving over to others the responsibility and power to extend God's kingdom. After having washed the feet of the apostles, Jesus tells them, "I shall no longer call you servants, because a servant does not know the master's business; I call you friends because I have made known to you everything I have learnt from my Father.... I chose you, and appointed you to go out and bear fruit...so that the Father will give you anything you ask him in my name" (John 15:15-16).

Jesus was a person of integrity, committed to doing what he believed was the right thing, regardless of the consequences. Consider, for example, his interaction with Pilate. Not cowed by Pilate's power to order his death, Jesus goes so far as to challenge the Roman Procurator: "You would have no power over me at all if it had not been given you from above" (John 19:11).

Christian leadership is essentially living as Jesus did. The wisdom people desire and recommend nothing more or less for anyone who purports to be a Christian leader. As we interviewed them, listened to their stories and their ideas for change, we recognized in their concept of leadership the model of Jesus we have just defined. This model is not confining or tightly prescriptive. It allows for personal variation in style and adaptation to specific roles and situations. The different ways in which Jesus is perceived as a leader are revealed in the metaphors which have been used to describe him: teacher, king, companion on the journey, master, miracle worker, healer, servant, shepherd, and prophet. All are accurate, all reveal different ways of describing his way of reaching people and moving things to action.

Recommendations for Christian Leaders

In each of the chapters which follow, we explore a characteristic of leadership based on the Jesus model and the expectations expressed by the wisdom people. They are people living full and active lives in the world, seeing leadership in its many forms, defining needs both personal and communal to which they hope leaders will respond, and shaping their own leadership style on their understanding of gospel values. They are, in fact, Christian leaders themselves though they carry no official titles. Comfortable with the strength that comes from

their own sense of leadership and power, they expect similar behaviors on the part of those filling church leadership roles. Over and
above all things, the wisdom people expect that Christian leaders will
have a deep personal relationship with the Lord and will attempt to
model their leadership on the Jesus they have personally encountered.
While there is no single way in which personal spirituality is revealed,
the credibility of Christian leadership rests on people's sensing
leaders' deep, personal faith and commitment.

Listen

Both the desire and the ability to listen is the foundation for all
ministry. It reveals the leader's wanting to learn and grow through
understanding the wisdom others offer. Listening implies dialogue,
the respectful exchange at the adult-to-adult level. It involves the
suspension of one's own viewpoint to attempt to truly hear and
understand another. Because listening is a complex process, leaders
need to develop their listening skills to be able to sort through all
they might hear to get at the essential truth of a situation. Listening
gives the leader access to people and their needs, hopes, weaknesses and strengths. It reveals the state of the community.

Establish a Vision

The second characteristic of effective leaders is the ability to help
the community articulate and commit to a vision. Visioning grows
out of listening. Visioning involves reflecting on the messages of
scripture and the messages of the community, distilling them to
describe a future state so clearly that others can, figuratively, see,
touch, and taste it. Excitement follows when people sense, for the
first time, something they had felt stirring within but had not expressed. For a group, a vision with a mission orientation serves as
the rallying cry to action.

Respond to the Alienated and Marginated

The Jesus revealed in the scriptures and proclaimed in post-
Vatican II documents possessed "a preferential option for the poor."
Effective Christian leaders are those who imitate this loving Christ
in their ministries by emphasizing concern for the *anawim*—the most
alienated and marginalized members in society. They reach out to
the poor and challenge their communities to do the same.

Expand the Concept of Ministry

Too often the term ministry is reserved only for those actions
which take place in the context of liturgical celebrations and

parochial activity. Effective Christian leaders have a more expansive concept of ministry. They are able to define and support the ministries of the marketplace, the home, and the neighborhood, challenging people to see these as venues for proclaiming the Gospel to the world.

Collaborate

Christian leaders who embrace and value collaborative approaches to ministry discover the power of involving others. The sum is so much greater than the parts. Collaborative leaders do not act in isolation. They are inclusive rather than exclusive in approach. They are willing to listen to and collaborate with those whose views and style may differ from their own. Being collaborative taps into the gifts of many people, fosters creativity, and achieves greater results.

Support the Gifts and Ministries of the Laity

Effective Christian leaders know their own gifts as well as their personal limitations. In addition, they are aware of the magnitude of gifts present in others, convinced that each person is both gifted and called. Through their attitudes and behaviors they communicate that conviction. They accept as one of their major responsibilities supporting each and every member of the Christian community to discover, develop, and use the distinctive gifts given him or her, especially in carrying out ministries in the world.

Respond to the Needs of the Christian Community

Christians are called to the fullness of a life in Christ and believe that community is a powerful vehicle for realizing their spiritual growth. That growth can only be fostered effectively, however, when their specific needs are known and addressed. Through the development of supportive environments, effective leaders can help people identify their needs. Through people-sensitive approaches, they can personally respond to those needs and also assure that there is a communal response.

Support the Influencers of Values

There are key people who influence the development of Christian values within a social unit, be it the family, school, or workplace. There are critical periods when values are shaped, such as during one's early years. And there are events which profoundly influence values. Some influences come from expected sources, such as the family members; others from surprising places, such as a neighbor or a peer at work. Effective Christian leaders identify the major influencers of values, providing them support and encouragement as they positively influence the development of Christian values.

Be People of Integrity

To live and act with integrity is a commitment of the will, the mind, and the heart to be honest in all that a person is and does. It is a quality revealed through behaviors and relationships. People interacting with leaders who reveal personal integrity see no discrepancy between what these leaders say and what they do. If there is validity to Marshall McLuhan's phrase, "the medium is the message", then the vessel which carries the gospel to the people must be an individual of utmost integrity. Action, consistent with one's stated beliefs, is the litmus test for integrity.

Be Generative

Generative leaders are other-directed as Jesus was. Their primary concern is to bring about positive change in the lives of individuals and the larger community. Generative leaders use themselves, their gifts, and their resources to respond wherever they perceive needs. Christian generativity is differentiated from humanitarianism by the individual's acting out of Christ-centered love. Nowhere does such generativity permit motivation based on personal power, vanity, social acceptance, or recognition.

Be Compassionate

One of the most compelling crucibles for testing the presence of generativity is to examine how compassionate a person is. Compassionate leaders have a capacity for both sympathy and empathy. They move beyond those to action, to lighten the pain being experienced by another. Their responsiveness is open and generous borne out of truly sharing the pain another is suffering.

Communicate Hope and Joy

We live in a world and a society in which hope and joy appear to be the exception rather than the rule. Effective leaders are those who experience Christian joy and hope in their own lives and are able to communicate this to others. They are not blind optimists nor Pollyannas. They realize the inevitability of pain in all lives; they see its integration into the growth process; they are able to reveal the gospel message of new life with authenticity even in the face of suffering.

Jesus: The Model for Christian Leaders

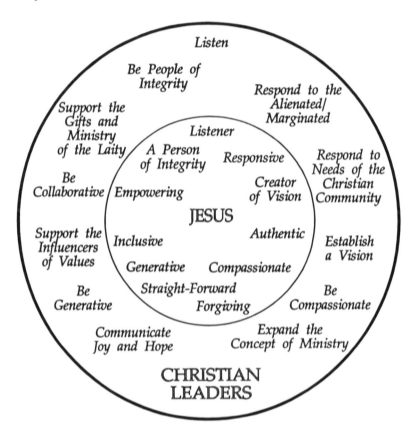

JESUS was a man of integrity, who was authentic, generative, compassionate, forgiving and straightforward.

As a minister, he listened to people, responded to what he heard, created and communicated a vision, included all in his community, and empowered people and communities to implement that vision.

The Christian leader is a person of integrity who is generative, compassionate and who communicates hope and joy.

The Christian leader listens to people, creates a vision with those people, responds to the needs of the Christian community, especially the alienated and marginalized, works collaboratively with others in responding to those needs, expands the concept of ministry, and supports the gifts and ministries of the laity and those who influence their values.

Conclusion

What is evident from our discussions with the wisdom people is that the characteristics of Jesus as a leader translate effectively into a model for Christian leadership. These are the characteristics which the wisdom people themselves strive to emulate in their own lives, in their own roles as leaders. Their life experiences and the ways in which they have responded have enabled them to grow and become role models for others. Their words and their wisdom can help other Christian leaders seeking personal, professional, and spiritual growth.

The diagram on page 40 shows the relationship between Jesus' characteristics as a leader and how these might be defined in terms of behaviors expected of contemporary leaders. Each of the twelve chapters which follows explores one of these in depth. The effective Christian leader is one who understands the relationships among these characteristics and attempts to integrate them all into his or her approach to leadership.

Reflection Questions

1. What do I perceive to be the major characteristics of Jesus as leader?

2. In what ways during the past week have I tried to live those same values?

3. What is the major aspect of leadership which I need to develop? How do I know that?

II
THE TASKS OF LEADERSHIP

JESUS AS LEADER	THE CHRISTIAN LEADER
Listened and responded to what he heard, and created and communicated a vision.	Listens to people and with them, creates a vision from what they have heard.
Was inclusive of all in that vision.	Works collaboratively with others in responding to the needs of the Christian community, especially those of its most alienated or marginalized members.
Empowered people to implement that vision.	Empowers others by fostering an expanded concept of ministry, especially one which supports the gifts and ministries of the laity and those who positively influence the development of Christian values.

3
Listening: The Basis of Effective Leadership

Be quick to listen, but slow to speak, slow to anger.
James 1:19

The gospels reveal fascinating insights into leadership: Pharisees who see life as a set of rules, Pilate who is intimidated by jealous leaders and the crowd, Judas who reaches for power and ends in despair, and apostles who are immobilized by the loss of their Master. Jesus, in contrast, models a dramatically different form of leadership. He stays in no fixed spot; he has no seat of power; he walks around listening and talking with people.

All that Jesus does is focused on people, hearing their questions, sharing their pain, and responding with both words and action. Love is the foundation for all that he does, and that love is nowhere more evident than in the way Jesus listens. He is direct and open with people, erecting no barriers between himself and those he meets. It is his listening that puts his leadership approach in sharp contrast to that taken by others in the gospel story. Jesus listens intently and responds compassionately. The Scriptures are replete with such examples. In the Gospel of John (chapter 11) Jesus listens to the plaintive cry of Mary grieving over the death of her brother, Lazarus. He is profoundly moved, his tears revealing the depth of his feelings, and he responds compassionately.

Everyone wants to be listened to, truly heard, responded to, and respected. Listening is the greatest compliment we can give, conveying to another person our interest in them and our concern for their

45

well-being. It is an absolute prerequisite for effective leadership because it is the primary mechanism for building relationships.

Listening as a Characteristic of All Leaders

Effective leaders understand the importance of listening. Donald Petersen, a former CEO of the Ford Motor Company quoted in an interview in *USA Today*, spoke of his experience with leaders and managers in the corporate world:

> Too many managers never listen to others. They think their role is to come up with some creative ideas, write down some actions so that people can implement them, call a meeting and say, "Here's what we're going to do, and here's who does each item." That'll get you only as far as your own mind can take you.

Two writers with a keen interest in leadership in the corporate world stress the essential nature of listening as a prerequisite for effective leadership. Warren Bennis and Burt Nanus describe leadership as a "transaction": the first component involves paying attention to others; then, listening to what they believe, need, and want; and, finally, communicating with them in such a way that they feel they have been heard, that they are in dialogue, and that a relationship has been established.

LISTENING AS A TRANSACTION

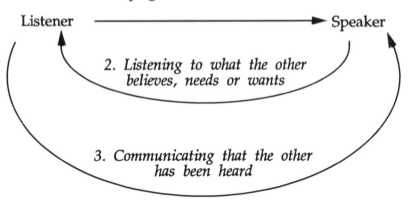

1. *Paying attention to the other*

Listener ⟶ Speaker

2. *Listening to what the other believes, needs or wants*

3. *Communicating that the other has been heard*

The same emphasis on the value of listening to be an effective leader is prominent in the writings of Father William Bausch, a noted author and pastor. He speaks of how he came to an awareness of the value of listening and, in the process, discovered that those to whom he listened had much more to offer than he expected:

> One clearly formative experience for me was acting as a priest-advisor to groups of couples involved in the Christian Family Movement. One rule at CFM meetings is that the priest can speak only during the last five minutes. I had no choice but to listen to the laity. I discovered that they had a remarkable spiritual strength which the particular struggles, sorrows, and joys of their lives taught them.

Like Bausch's experience, the process of listening which we used in doing the research for this book was truly a transforming experience. As we played and replayed the tapes made during the sessions, we found ourselves appreciating and respecting people more with each listening. We found a wealth of wisdom and holiness residing in the people of God. The sadness is that these same people (whom we believe are representative of the larger church population) have rarely or never been asked to share their wisdom. Few of the interviewees reported any religious leaders who had gone out of their way to convey an interest in hearing what they think, feel, believe, hope for, and experience.

The more church leaders follow the example of Bausch and develop their capacity to listen to the "remarkable spiritual strength…and the struggles, sorrows and joys" of the laity, the more effective they will be. Some wisdom people ascribe the declining numbers in many churches to leaders' failure to listen. As we noted above, listening is a transaction. It involves not only paying attention to others and their needs and beliefs, but also communicating to them that they have been heard. If all the elements of listening are not present, leaders appear to be out of touch with people's needs. They exacerbate the decline of the very institution they are trying to promote. Unless leaders listen in a way that conveys to others attention and respect, they may discover that they have no followers.

The Wisdom People as Listeners

Our assessment of the wisdom people is that they are listened to because they themselves listen. They are receptive rather than judgmental. They want to know what others think and feel. Listening is clearly a major value in their lives.

Anthony, a doctor who described himself as a "marginal Catholic," revealed an almost obsessive need to listen to people in order "to understand them and their needs." In describing his own approach, he spoke of trying to discover what he can about each patient, not only in terms of their medical problems but in terms of their total life view. His commitment to listening is also a form of self-discipline. Anthony realizes that he has very strong beliefs and he fears that a failure to really listen might result in his imposing those beliefs on others. He also knows that, as a doctor, he may exert undue influence on those facing critical decisions. His listening is essential to his responding both professionally and ethically.

Scott, a community organizer committed to helping the oppressed better their lives, talked about his desire to understand the people with whom he works. He has a fervent yearning "to find out what is special about each person, what are their special needs, their special contributions, their special gifts." His listening allows him to encounter others in a new way and leads to a deep appreciation of the uniqueness of each individual.

What Scott hopes to uncover through his intense listening is not just the needs of the other person, but the gifts which they have to offer. Through his listening, he helps people to understand and appreciate those gifts. Thus, he empowers people, giving them confidence and energy to use their gifts to deal with challenges in their own lives and those of others. Helping them to uncover their uniqueness, he fosters self-esteem and a sense of personal power that they can appreciate and celebrate. Raymond, another of the wisdom people, reflects this same value of listening. Hoping to empower others through his listening, he simply states, "If I don't understand your problem, I can't help you to help yourself."

Effective Leaders Master the Art of Listening

Given the value which the wisdom people place on listening, it is not surprising that they strongly urge Christian leaders to develop that capacity. One after another pleads for leaders who are committed to listening and for a church which attempts to listen as Jesus did:

- "We need the support of a very active listening church."

- "The hierarchy and the [ministers] need to start listening to the pain of the people."
- "People have real needs, real fears, real desires and religious leaders cannot remain aloof...listening is important."
- "I wonder sometimes if ministers realize the conditions under which some of their parishioners live. I wonder if they're really aware of the many stresses."
- "They've got to pay a little more attention to the needs, the real needs of the people, and allow more freedom of expression and attitudes. You can't pour everybody into a mold."
- "I feel very disenfranchised because they are not listening to me. They have no idea what my struggles are."

We believe that these statements and pleas are not isolated comments of negative, overly-critical people. Rather, they are representative of the concerns and hopes of committed Christians who are convinced of the direct relationship between listening and effective leadership. They identify a number of reasons for recommending that leaders develop their listening ability: only leaders who listen will be able to communicate to others that they are understood; understanding leads to increased compassion, and compassion results in effective ministry. Finally, if the church is not experienced as a listening church, it will lose its credibility and potential as a major force for good in people's lives and the life of the broader community.

Barriers to Listening

Effective leaders either instinctively know the importance of listening or they have learned its importance through experience. Given this reality, why are there so many people who do not experience a sense of being heard by church leaders? With the model of Jesus as the compassionate listener, what is it that blocks leaders from taking a similar approach? What is it that keeps them from appreciating listening as the way of building relationships between themselves and others? Of the myriad of answers to these questions, we believe the major barriers are:

- Listening does not serve the leader's personal need.
  Because behavior is need-directed, a common cause

of not listening is that leaders find what others say threatening to their own sense of security and self-esteem.

- They simply do not know how to listen. Too often they assume that if they hear someone speak, they are listening. Or, perhaps they have been taught to listen too literally, hearing the denotation but not the connotation, hearing words but missing the real message.
- The model of leadership to which they were introduced established the view that, as leaders, they are expected to have the answers. Not having a ready reply erodes their self-confidence.
- They are in a community which has never had a sense of its own responsibility to speak up and so has surrendered its responsibility to express its own needs.
- They believe that listening is unnecessary, that their life experience is sufficient for deciding on a course of action.
- They listen to gain support for a course of action they already have in mind rather than as a way of learning the true needs to which their plan of action should respond.
- They feel threatened by diversity and fail to appreciate the value of viewpoints and life experiences different from their own.

What the wisdom people recommend is that listening, taken in the narrow sense of hearing someone speak, is not enough. There have been, for example, concerted efforts within the last decade by church leaders to establish "listening sessions" ostensibly to provide forums where they would have an opportunity to hear from the people of God. Some people find these sessions unsatisfactory, even a sham, when the leaders fail to convey that they really want to listen, using the event only as a way to justify their pre-existing viewpoints.

Effective leaders listen to the needs and hungers which underlie what is being said and, most importantly, respond in such a way that the speaker feels he or she has been understood and has had an impact. This kind of active listening does not imply agreement with what is said, but it does build relationship so that ongoing dialogue and resolution of differences are possible.

The failure to listen invites a host of difficulties for those in leadership roles. They are perceived as out of touch with the group; their decisions are suspect or seen as dictatorial; their strongest members move away from them, alienated by a sense of impotence in the face of such arrogance; they are surrounded instead by those who tolerate their ineptness. Increasingly, they find that they have fewer people to lead and influence.

Listening as the Key to Understanding

The process of listening leads to understanding the aspirations, needs, and hurts of others. Only when people feel that they have been listened to and that the listener truly wants to understand their reality, can a mutually respectful relationship result.

Lee is one of those people who possesses the rare gift of articulating reality in its simplest form:

> Give people what they want. Find out what they need. Be more responsive to the individual needs of people. I don't think the clergy realize the hardships that people have. I think they're blind to the fact of a lot of people's problems. They don't have time to go one-on-one with people. I think they don't have time to minister to people, because they're too busy doing ministry.

Her ability to reduce effective ministry to its most basic components is refreshing: realize how little you know, listen to people and find out what they really need, and then respond by giving people what they need to grow.

Since interviewing Lee we have frequently quoted her when addressing groups of professional ministers. Her comment that ministers are "so busy doing ministry that they don't have time to minister to people," inevitably draws embarrassed laughter. Most of the audience is painfully aware that she has convincingly described their experience: they have become so involved in the administrative and organizational aspects of leadership that they rarely have time to be present to people and to listen to them.

Kate, speaking from her experience as mother, wife, media specialist, and social activist, lamented the apparent lack of understanding of life's realities on the part of many in church leadership. She talked especially about the burden and stress of working mothers and of unmarried, pregnant teen-age girls. "Nobody's listening to these people." The result, she is convinced, is that ministers tend to preach ideals which are unattainable, out of touch with the capability of those to whom they speak. Consequently, instead of experiencing an understanding, compassionate, loving church, people come away with a sense of condemnation, frustration, and guilt. The unattainable, proposed as the norm, portrays the leader as out of touch and is alienating to people.

A different perspective concerning the church's not listening is revealed in a story told by Kevin. As a young married man and new father, he was struggling financially, holding two jobs to make ends meet. He noted that many others in the congregation were under similar pressures. By his own admission, Kevin was a Sunday Christian, probably attending more out of habit than strong conviction, but nevertheless a member of the parish. One Sunday he heard that there would a regular second collection to pay for a $100,000 organ which the church was acquiring. He left angry, troubled by the apparent lack of concern shown by the church's leadership to the very real struggles which people were having. In this case, it might have been appropriate for the church to buy the organ. Unfortunately, the image projected was one of indifference to the needs of many people.

Compassion: The Response to True Listening

To be compassionate leaders, we must become listening leaders. Only when church leaders listen intently to people, members and non-members, will they be in a position to respond constructively as Jesus would. When people do not feel listened to and taken seriously, they come away with a sense of being devalued and disenfranchised.

Jack summons up the image of Jesus, the listener, as the compassionate one who conveyed to people that he was truly with them. Highlighting the explicit correlation between listening and a compassionate response, Jack challenges church leaders to evaluate their willingness to listen and their corresponding capacity to be compassionate.

> We're supposed to be a compassionate church. Jesus was compassionate. He listened to people. He listened to the women in the scripture who came to talk with him....I think we are doing a great disservice in that I think if we talked to our people and listened to

our people, really listened to them, I think we would learn so much more.

Interestingly, as we spoke with the wisdom people and asked them about their sources of support, almost no one indicated that they would turn to church leaders. Their conclusion was that people in authority are not really interested and simply would not understand the day-to-day challenges they face.

Listening as a Prerequisite for Credibility

Chris, a manager with broad authority who has had his own share of challenges running a business and trying to serve the needs of his staff, speaks repeatedly of the unequivocal need to develop religious leaders who value listening. His conviction is that some of the most effective religious leaders are lay people who are "out in the trenches," because it is through their listening and their personal witness that they reach others. Further, he believes it is the responsibility of higher level leaders "...bishops, etc., to find ways to tap that potential and listen to these people."

Chris emphasizes his concern that the church will lose its credibility if, while not listening to its members, it projects an image of excessive concern for the internal needs of the organization rather than a genuine concern for the needs of people.

> There is a spiritual hunger in the world and people are not looking to the churches to have that hunger met. One of the major reasons why people are not looking to the churches is that they are often seen as largely irrelevant. They are not listening to people, nor do they seem to be interested in the real needs of people. They seem to be obsessed with the inner workings of the institutional church.

Chris is convinced that religion ultimately has the answers to today's critical societal issues which "are destructive to individuals and families." His fear is that if the church does not develop a stance of truly wanting to listen to the struggles and needs of people, they will not turn to the church for the support and help they require. For Chris, the church will be most effective in conveying its spiritual message when people are clearly able to detect the relationship between religion and their personal spirituality. Too often religion, defined in terms of organization, structure, and guidelines, is perceived as irrelevant, even as people search for a spirituality which will sustain them.

It is the substance of dialogue and listening that Chris is referring to. His remarks recall a conversation, reported in *Contemplative Prayer* between Thomas Merton and the Dali Lama who said that Catholics do not talk about their prayer life but about the institution. Buddhists, on the other hand, talk about central issues. Our bias all too often is to focus on rules and structures rather than on beliefs and how they relate to the essential dimensions of our lives.

Sharon was the only interviewee who identified herself as having been a church minister, at one point having served as a professional liturgist in a parish. She believes she would approach ministry very differently today, based on her experience in the business world. "I wouldn't have such high expectations of people anymore." She is much more aware and sensitive to the demands which family and work life place on people. "I would listen more to what their needs are." Speaking of her own development and learning, Sharon makes an interesting distinction when she says that in the past she used to do "good liturgy." Today she would approach it very differently. Having listened to the stories of the parishioners, she would allow liturgy to emerge from the needs and viewpoints they describe, making the liturgy a true community celebration. The focus would be on people's needs, not on a prescriptive approach driven by liturgical correctness.

She offers a very practical suggestion for creating an environment for listening and dialogue:

> I think what might be a great idea is if clergy and staff could somehow through the course of the year gather people and have supper with them. Talk with them. Ask them what it is like out there. Get a real feel for what people are experiencing out there in their day-to-day lives, out in the workplace. Then, just plainly ask them: "What do you need to hear from us? What are we not telling you?"

Relationship: The Heart of Listening

Establishing and maintaining a relationship is at the heart of listening. Typically, only when positive relationships exist are people able to take risks with what they might say, to be open to reveal their own vulnerability, and to identify their needs. A relationship creates a foundation of mutual respect and openness. It allows differences to be explored, resulting in growth for both sides. Listening also requires patience because people often do not have the words ready to convey the depth of their feelings.

While there must be mutuality in the relationship, it is incumbent on leaders to establish the basis on which the parties can communicate. They are vested with more power because of the role they are called to fill. Generally, leaders are expected to create the context in which human exchange will occur. How they signal their receptiveness to truly listen to others will determine a large part of the leaders' success.

Conclusion

The message is clear and unambiguous. If you want to be an effective leader, LISTEN.

If the church hopes to energize the laity to carry the gospel message to the world, its leaders must do more than just passively listen. They must actively be involved with people, truly hearing their needs, and then responding to people's hungers—hungers placed within them by the Spirit of the Lord.

Listening is the foundation upon which all leadership is developed. As we will see in the next chapter, effective Christian leaders communicate the extent to which they have listened by helping to develop and articulate a vision which reflects what has been heard.

Reflection Questions

1. Am I convinced that listening is an absolute prerequisite for effective Christian leadership?

2. How would the people I serve evaluate my capacity for listening?

3. What do I do to develop a greater capacity for listening?

4
Vision: The Future Dimension of Leadership

Your kingdom come, your will be done on earth....
Matthew 6:10

"Where there is no vision the people perish!" This wisdom from Proverbs is as true for Christian leaders as it was for the people of the Old Testament when it was first uttered.

Vision is the spirit behind an organization; it is the energizing principle because it defines the desired future state which motivates a group, calling them to action. A vision asks, "Where is it that we want to go? What is it that we want to achieve?" Vision is not to be confused with a group's *mission* which addresses why an organization exists and describes its function. Rather, vision is the goal toward which people are moving.

Having worked as facilitators in both the business world and the institutional church, we start from a simple premise: church organizations, including dioceses, parishes, and groups, are no different from any other—they languish when they fail to establish a vision which is shared, clear, realistic, and dynamic. These four aspects of vision are critical to success. We need to caution that we are not simply speaking of drafting a vision statement, though that may be part of a group's process. Vision is an in-depth understanding of where a group is going. While its essence may be captured in a few words, it is something much broader. It is not simply a view of the future in which today's problems are solved. Rather, vision seeks a different reality: it focuses on future opportunity and transformation. Consider, for example, the quotation from the Lord's

56

Prayer which opens this chapter and might serve as Jesus' simple but profound vision statement. It describes the desired future state when God's kingdom will be achieved and his plan for creation realized. Behind these few words is a large body of faith and teachings believers can draw on to support them day-to-day as they work to achieve that kingdom.

Shared Vision

In his highly acclaimed work, *The Fifth Discipline*, Peter Senge speaks compellingly about the need for shared vision. Each member of a group has a personal vision of what he or she believes the group should achieve. Some of these visions are limited, others are broad, still others are unrealistic. Each is shaped by the individual's perceptions of the purpose and strength of the group and the abilities of its members. Shared vision results when individuals come together and determine what they, as a group, are committed to. It is achieved through the process of dialogue, allowing personal views to surface so that a shared vision might emerge to energize the entire group. Senge differentiates commitment from compliance. All too often, he suggests, members of a group comply with a vision defined by someone else. They may support it, but they are not truly committed ("joined" or "connected" is the etymological root) to it. It is not their energizing principle.

Too often, visions formulated in the privacy of a staff or team meeting or, even worse, in isolation by a leader, languish as unfulfilled dreams because the people they are to motivate do not own them. The only effective visions are those built on the contributions of as many people as possible. In addition, vision sharing must be a continuing process, both for the deeper understanding of those who prepared it and for others who may join them later. To be truly energizing, vision should be ever-present in people's minds, always pointing the way and giving hope.

Clear

Without clarity unnecessary confusion and even conflict may develop over varying interpretations of what a vision means as a guide for action. All too often we read vision statements which are lengthy, attempt to embrace too many concepts, and use religious jargon which obfuscates what could be stated much more simply and clearly. Typically, these are the statements that try to "cover the waterfront" so that no cause is overlooked and no group feels slighted. Visions of this sort are remembered by no one.

Realistic

Any organization or group which establishes an unattainable vision condemns itself to frustration and failure. Unrealistic visions are borne either from a group's not understanding its own strengths and weaknesses or from the mistaken hope that embracing an ambitious vision will somehow generate the necessary talent to fulfill it. If people sense that the vision is beyond their reach, they typically retreat, not wanting to be part of something that will founder.

Being realistic concerning vision involves an assessment of what the group can likely accomplish within a certain period of time. We learn to walk in faltering steps. Later we can run. Ultimately, we can think about a marathon.

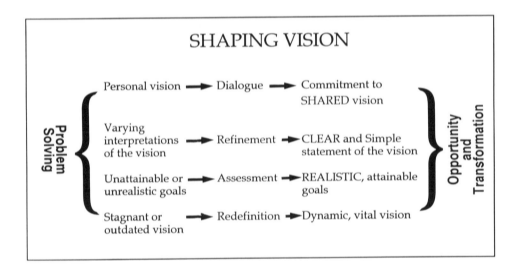

Dynamic

Visions which remain unchanged lose their vitality. It is through use and redefinition that they are kept alive and energizing. Typically, groups consider their vision when they first organize or when a new leader is named. They go through the hard work of developing a shared vision, and then move into action, failing to link all they do to the vision. Time passes and the group discovers that the vision is "outdated"; yesterday's vision is today's old news.

A dynamic vision is not one which shifts with each slight breeze of change, but one which takes into account new demands, redefined needs, and the changing external environment. The group's values are the constants which steer the vision. The vision itself is ever evolving to better define expectations for the future.

Distinctiveness of Christian Visions

While the vision for any organization must be shared, clear, realistic, and dynamic, vision for a Christian organization needs two additional characteristics: it must be gospel-based, and mission-oriented. The wisdom people are passionate in stating their recommendations to Christian leaders regarding these. They point out that whether a vision is written or not, one can sense its focus by pinpointing where a group gives its greatest attention and puts its energy. Too often, they feel organizations are focused more on maintenance and preservation of the institution than on fostering the Christ's mission. Finally, they point out that visions frequently lack a mission dimension; they do not respond adequately to the pressing needs of our time.

Leaders and Vision

Vision is a corporate involvement, but the role of the group leader is essential in two dimensions. First, the leader supports the group as it defines where it wants to go. This is done largely through the listening process we discussed in the previous chapter: hearing the needs, hungers, hopes, and aspirations of people, the leader helps them to see a different end-state to which they might move.

Second, the leader is the challenger and change agent, helping the group assess how it is achieving its vision and supporting the group's efforts to keep the vision current.

With our discussion of what constitutes a vision, we turn to what the wisdom people have to say about issues they believe church groups should consider as they debate and define their visions. These issues are illustrative, provided neither as an exhaustive list nor as a mandatory one because each vision must be distinctive to the individual group. It is the group itself that best understands its needs and the issues which confront its members and their neighbors. What the words of the wisdom people do, therefore, is challenge groups to examine the broader environment of which they are a part, and to shape their responses to major spiritual and societal issues.

Effective Christian Leaders Are Focused on Mission Rather Than Maintenance

The wisdom people are unequivocal in expressing their frustration with the fact that the primary energy of the Christian community is directed to issues of maintenance rather than being directed to the accomplishment of Christ's mission. They single out the time and effort that is expended on relatively insignificant aspects of internal church concerns. As one of them comments, communities "seem more concerned with who can do what on the altar than with the fact that there are people dying from want of food and from oppressive and unjust structures." As they make recommendations to Christian leaders, it is evident that these people, with their commitment to the gospel, would be much more supportive of the church if they saw it having a vital, gospel-based focus. A number talk candidly about their ambivalence toward the institutional church, saddened by the diversion of substantial human and financial resources toward maintaining the institution. Their concern mirrors that of theologian Avery Dulles who lamented in an article in *America* that the Catholic church, for example, is developing to a point of "ecclesiocentrism."

> The church has become too introverted. The Catholic church is highly sacramental, institutional, and hierarchical in its structures. Its activities are primarily directed toward the institution and pastoral care of its own members, whose needs and demands tax the institution to its limits.

If the people we interviewed are truly representative of the larger Christian population, the church is not only losing the commitment of some of its most powerful members, it is also alienating potential leaders needed now and in the future.

Mark, an executive of a large organization, provides insight as to why this alienation may be taking place. When speaking to a group of business leaders, he talked about his own company's commitment to growth as essential for its continued vitality. If they were not focused on growth, people could easily slip into doing the less important, less challenging tasks. Such behaviors encourage ennui and alienation, cause interpersonal relations to deteriorate, and ultimately, erode the organization.

> Our company is committed to growth. The best justification for growth is that an organization that doesn't grow becomes static and sluggish. People in a static or sluggish organization become mean-spirited. Individuals become frustrated with the resulting loss of commitment and, ultimately, the departure of talented people.

The key learning from Mark's statement is the importance of a central motivator within the vision. For his organization, it is growth. For another, it might be how to adapt itself to serve a changing population. For a third, it might be rebuilding confidence with the public after a previous leadership team allowed relationships to deteriorate. The point is that the vision must have an overarching focus which sets the direction for the organization. It defines the desired future state that committed people want to achieve, allowing them to concentrate their energies on the planning and dedicated hard work that will help to get them there.

We have selected five wisdom people who provide compelling viewpoints concerning the importance of mission-focus: Scott, a community organizer, attempting to support the interests of poor, immigrant restaurant workers; Chris, a publisher, whose concern is the inward focus of the church; Hillman, a state legislator, committed to creating socially responsive law to improve the lives of the less fortunate; Dawne, an administrative assistant, who is concerned about the kind of church communities we build; and Kaylujan, also a legislator, who speaks of the church's role in driving social change through the witness and action of its members. Interestingly, each speaks from the viewpoint of his or her own occupation and experience, yet there are common themes running through their remarks.

Scott's involvement in community organization affords him frequent opportunities to work with leaders of numerous religious groups. His personal religious journey led him through a labyrinth of denominations, resulting in a unique perspective for evaluating the strengths and shortcomings of churches. His recommendations regarding the development of an animating vision contain three major elements. First, like Mark, he emphasizes the aspect of growth and mission. Second, he says a fundamental aspect of vision should be the development of leaders—in other words, an organization should be self-perpetuating with an eye to the future. Third, he speaks of a vision which commits to attempting new approaches, rather than being contented with the safe and secure.

Scott's philosophy is probably best summed up with his statement, "Growth is the only evidence of life. I would say for there to be life, there has to be growth." He is not simply talking about numerical size, though that is an important indicator of whether a vision is truly responsive to people's needs. He is talking about the focus of an organization and its members: to put their energies where they will have maximum impact on both their personal transformation as well as the needs they serve. Growth, in this sense, is the creative response to hearing a need, creating a vision for the future, and mobilizing to achieve it.

Scott, impressed with one church's exceptional growth in membership, asked how it had come about. "This is not a church," he was told, "this is a mission. Once we become a church, we begin to die." The implication is clear: if the primary focus becomes the church itself, atrophy sets in. When energy is directed outward rather than inward, the result is life-giving. This view is corroborated by many of the interviewees who are dissatisfied with their present churches because their pulling away from a mission focus is sapping their life and vitality. Programs and activities are more often directed to the needs of the membership rather than toward the goal of transforming society. The same issue exists beyond the local parish. Pope John Paul II voiced his concern to American bishops that religious congregations in the United States seem more concerned with the needs of their members than the needs of the people they are sent to serve.[1] The basic question which should confront both leaders and groups is whether their vision looks inward or outward.

From his community experience, Scott recognizes the need for member development as a way of moving a vision to fulfillment. This starts with identifying members who will give life to the institution and then supporting and training them to take on leadership roles.

> There has to be an investment in people and particularly in developing their members to be apostles to go forth and be fishers of men and women.

This kind of development pays rich dividends. Scott speaks of the proselytizing of some of the evangelical churches as evidence of what individual development can achieve. He credits their success to the fact that they have leaders and members willing to go out to the larger community proclaiming their message. He likened their approach to what has proved successful in his own organizing. He identifies people who are most successful in recruiting new members. The successful recruiters are dubbed "fishers of men and women." Organizers have perhaps embraced the scriptural concept more readily than many church leaders.

Finally, Scott made a recommendation which is echoed by other wisdom people: "Get off your butts!" If you want to have a church of mission rather than maintenance, "Get out there and mix it up, start things, do things, experiment." The vital, successful churches, from his perspective, will be those that are not satisfied with the status quo but are willing to risk, try new approaches and develop visions which reflect a sense of urgency and mission.

Scott's own model is St. Paul, a man who lived his life with intense passion and zeal. If Paul were in ministry today, Scott suggests, people would probably criticize his failure to lead a balanced life because he was a man on fire with a mission. "That's what it took to get the church started," and that fire may be what is needed today to energize the church. Scott's remarks confirm what Tom Peters, the author of the best-selling *In Search of Excellence*, recommended to a group of priests interested in the issue of evangelization, "Be a fanatic with a vision!"[2]

Chris, whose professional life involves him with organizational and business issues, sees the limitations of the church when it focuses too much on its own operations and not on its broader objectives. Like Scott, Chris speaks with passion about his conviction that a more pastoral, mission-oriented vision is needed in the church:

> I have a great deal of love and respect for the institutional church, but it needs a kick in the fanny in order to live the gospel. I am concerned that there is sometimes a loss of the sense of the gospel because of the need on the part of leadership to maintain the institution.

It is the excessive amount of resources that go into status-quo-thinking and action that keeps the church from its broader role of reaching out beyond its own organizational boundaries:

The maintenance attitude is what's keeping the
church from being relevant. It's draining the energy
for ministry and pastoral response. The institutional
church is too focused on being what it once was and
not open enough to being what it can be, what it
should be. As a result, the world is moving past the
church and the church is playing catch up all the time
and not responding to people's needs. People need to
find out that the gospel and the spiritual dimension
of religious life can offer them some succor and help
them reach richer, fuller lives. Many no longer look
to the church for that or simply go through Sunday
participation but get no satisfaction. No one is leading them to see what is there.

Chris's remarks recall the words of Peter Senge cited earlier
concerning vision: too often the focus is on solving current problems
and, in the process, missing out on the opportunities which lie ahead.
The critique that Chris offers comes from someone who has a deep
love for the church but experiences great frustration when he realizes
that people's hungers can be met only by a church which is actively
and aggressively living and spreading the Lord's message. If he saw
a greater faithfulness to this mission orientation, he admits that he
himself would be a much more committed member. He is not at-
tracted by an organization whose energy is being depleted by constant, almost compulsive obsession with issues "around the altar"
rather than responding to the pressing unmet needs of the world.

The third viewpoint is that of Hillman, who speaks from the
perspective of being a legislator and the son of a minister. He
observes, "Over the past several years, many ministers and the
memberships of congregations have been confined to the work of
the congregation as opposed to reaching out." He believes this
excessive internal focus is severely hampering the ability of the
church to carry out its mission effectively. He challenges the church
to appreciate the unique gift it possesses to respond to the spiritual
and moral hungers of God's people.

Don't be afraid to explain the word and take the word
outside the four walls of the church, because you
have something they are dying to hear. There is a
burning desire to know more about Christianity, the
values, the teachings of Christ.

The effectiveness of the church is directly related to how it handles the tension between two roles. On the one hand, it exists to be a consistent and stabilizing voice, to teach, and to pass on the tenets of faith. On the other, it must constantly redefine the very things it stands for, demonstrating their relevance to contemporary culture and providing leadership to address today's issues. The vision, to effectively foster the mission of Jesus Christ, must be oriented to the present while being true to the group's long-standing values. Approaches which were effective in the past may not be relevant or effective today.

In recent years, with our increasing sensitivity to issues of diversity, much has been written about religious inculturation, the ability to apply religious values to the reality of a particular group or culture. Religion cannot be indiscriminately thrust upon people without cognizance of or sensitivity to their needs and their culture. Such was the insensitivity of some early missionary activity in the Americas. We have come to realize how destructive such an approach can be, not only to the different culture but to the development and growth of a vibrant Christianity. Thus, one of religion's challenges is to determine what is required within a particular culture to allow its message to be heard. The result should ultimately be that culture and religion are both strengthened because of their interaction; they come to be seen as allies and not as adversaries.

For Hillman, his role is the translation of the gospel messages he heard from his father into an action plan: trying to drive systemic change within society. He is fighting for laws which mirror gospel values, and he works to convince his peers that those are the kinds of bills they should support. He may not be explicit about the gospel on the floor of the assembly, but the messages which he is delivering flow directly from his understanding of the scripture. His challenge to the church is no different from that to his fellow legislators. He wants to see a strong social commitment to have "God's kingdom come," to be a reality in terms of justice and human dignity.

As Dawne reflects on the church, she speaks in almost visionary terms, but she is clearly rooted in reality. Like Scott and Hillman, she has a strong commitment to the church's role of transforming society. Her perspective is that the church functions as a safe place for people to explore their beliefs so that they might live vibrant Christian lives in the world.

> It is difficult...to articulate our values...to continual-
> ly be reviewing them. It is difficult, mulling them

over anew, to see how they have changed if we don't have someone to share them with.... The church is a very safe place to do that, or can be. I guess that I would like to see our churches as safe havens, as places where we cancome together, not only to share our answers but to share our questions. I don't think that we question enough. And I do think the answers lie within us as long as we get all the bits and pieces from each other.

Dawne's viewpoint concerning "safe havens" is not contradictory to the theme of outward focus. It is the balancing of the inward and the outward, recognizing that people need to strengthen their own beliefs and commitments so that they can transform the world.

Kaylujan's remarks complement Dawne's as she speaks of the role of her church in supporting people, like herself, to live their Christian values through their work and communities. A tough-minded, practical legislator, Kaylujan is brief in capturing what the church's role is in the lives of the congregation.

For me, life is living out what I hear here at church. I mean *living* what goes on here—if I can carry that out in my lifestyle and what I do, what actions I take, and what I say. Every member who comes here has an impact where they work. And they are the sum total of themselves and what they pick up here. They keep starting out, spreading out like a ripple, and it keeps on going...and...[has] an impact where they are in the world. I hope so!

Her words speak to the integration of church and work life for her and other parish members. So deeply did she believe this that, as we spoke, her tone bordered on impatience with the suggestion that anyone could think differently, that they could see a separation between what they address on Sunday mornings and what they address during the work week. Her experience of church and how it supports her in her professional role, is not shared by many of the wisdom people. The chasm is too broad between what is seen as important and stressed in church, and what is important in the lives of the members and the community. All too often we heard frustration at that gap.

Scott, Chris, Hillman, Dawne, and Kaylujan are representative ofother wisdom people and are unequivocal in their messages: if the church is to carry out faithfully its God-given purpose, it must develop a mission-oriented vision which informs and guides all that it does.

Conclusion

Vision, in the way in which we have presented it, is the energizing force for any church group, provided it is shared and serves as the underpinning for all that the group does. A primary role of leaders, regardless of where they are placed in the organization, is to listen to people both within and outside the church so that they might support the development of a vision which will drive individual and group action and behavior. Vision takes into account the distinctiveness of the community, embracing its diversity as a strength. It is modeled on the approach of Jesus: the kingdom of God is open to all, ultimately it can only be realized if all are part of it. Guided by challenges such as those offered by the wisdom people, vision addresses the needs of the group and of the broader community. It ultimately leads to the realization of the kingdom of God.

Reflection Questions

1. Does the group which I lead have a vision statement that is shared, clear, realistic, and dynamic?

2. Is the vision one which challenges me, stretches me?

3. Am I confident that all the members of the group, congregation, organization, etc. are aware of the group's vision and able to discuss it?

4. Is the vision inwardly or outwardly focused?

Notes

[1] Letter dated February 22, 1989 from Pope John Paul II to the bishops of the United States, responding to the report of the commission established to study the state of religious life in the United States.

[2] Reported to us by Father Patrick Brennan, the Director of the Office of Evangelization of the Archdiocese of Chicago.

5

Gospel Imperatives:
The Locus of Leadership

Then, fixing his eyes on his disciples [Jesus] said, How
blessed are you....

Luke 6:20

We talked in the two previous chapters about listening and the development of a shared vision as processes in which the Christian leader plays a key role. Absorbing what is said and supporting the group as it defines a future desired state are activities that require his or her active and ongoing support. But leadership demands something more if leaders are to follow the Jesus leadership model: they must challenge those they lead with new ideas, fresh viewpoints, ethical standards, and an in-depth understanding of gospel values. In the absence of these, their leadership is empty, their role merely that of synthesizer of what others have said.

What, then, are some of the challenges that leaders should raise with their groups? To help discern the direction of vision and mission for the church on the eve of the twenty-first century, wisdom people identify what they believe were Jesus's priorities and what should, therefore, be the priorities of Christian leaders today. Their responses, interestingly, can be enunciated as a kind of contemporary litany of beatitudes. Blessed are those leaders who:

- respond to the needs of the poor
- promote peace
- share the wealth
- confront the "isms"
- foster the rights of women
- challenge social ills
- empower people

From the viewpoint of the wisdom people, these beatitudes are crucial for leaders if they are to attract followers and be effective in promoting the gospel at this time and in this culture. Nowhere did they suggest that the leadership role is easy. They expressed compassion for leaders who are faced with complex problems and challenges. But at the same time, they were also critical of leaders, suggesting that not dealing with broader issues actually multiplies the problems themselves and erodes leadership influence.

The Courage toBe Radical

It was primarily in the area of social justice that the wisdom people concentrated their remarks. Recommendations regarding the need for gospel-focused leaders and a more gospel-oriented vision elicited some of the most critical comments. The stories the wisdom people told and their recommendations suggest that these are vital, absorbing, and challenging issues for them as they go about their work. They look for leadership support, recognizing that only through a unified response will these issues be effectively addressed.

Frat, like so many others, talks of his love for the church but expresses his frustration with its seeming lethargy and willingness to maintain the status quo:

> I'm not anxious to tear down the church. I want the church to be what Jesus wanted it to be. If Jesus came back to earth he would be outraged at the church that we have established in his name which reflects almost identically the church which was existing when he came. And he tore that one apart.

In what way does my vision for the church resemble the vision Jesus had for the church?

Marge relates a very graphic and touching story of attempting to locate housing for an abused woman and her child who had been evicted from their home.

> She called me on Good Friday and said, "I need a place to stay." I said, "Good Friday, piece of cake, no problem." And so I went from spot to spot to spot, and no one offered any help. I remember going to one church and their saying, "We have church services to attend to. Come back on Monday; maybe we can do something then. We haven't got time for this non-

sense right now." She found a friend of hers who was a lesbian, she finally found her a spot. You're right there in the gospel story; you are part of it and you need to see your place in that.

What she described as a gospel story is surely the present day recounting of the parable of the Good Samaritan. The churches, busy with the ritual of Good Friday, had no time to tend to the needs of the poor. Instead, it was today's Samaritan, the lesbian, who provided the support and the Christian response. Marge adds, "One of the things we don't teach people is how to be risk-takers, to step out on a limb. We teach them how to conform and stay in line."

She ponders what might have happened if the ministers she contacted on Good Friday had acted differently. She speculates on the witness such a radical gospel response would have given to their congregations and the larger community aware of the women's plight.

Do I have the courage to be radical? Does my concern for smooth operations keep me from taking risks?

A Gospel Vision

From his experience as a consultant in developing countries, Arthur reflects on the erosion of the church's credibility and effectiveness not only in places with seemingly overwhelming needs but within the society where local groups operate. He believes the church has to be "more pro-active, get out there in front and take the risk now." He is convinced that failure to take a more vigorous approach now will have dire consequences for the future of the church. He believes it is imperative that the church move beyond its protective stance.

> The organizational church has to take social risks.... This organizational church, and I make a distinction between the organizational church and the believing community, has always followed society. It hasn't very often led. It hasn't gone out on a limb. The church has to lead society ...in the importance of dealing with the poor, in solidarity with the poor ...in all social issues.

In what ways is my vision more influenced by society than by the gospel?
Do I foster a vision which requires risk and initiative?

An Assertive Role

The wisdom people expect that Christian leaders will be more aggressive in taking risks for the sake of the church's mission, for its own members, and for the people it serves. They identify specific areas where they hope the church will assume this more assertive role. Chief among their priorities is the area of social ministries, especially in responding to the needs of the materially poor.

Colman, committed to being a voice for the oppressed and marginalized, suggests that this should be the fundamental role of the church. Its mission is to be the voice and advocate of the poor, directing its resources to help people live a full life. He describes his own role as a Christian and a journalist attempting to do what few others in his profession see as a priority.

> I try to write about people who have been victimized —of course without being terribly morose about it, the outcasts, the marginals, the voiceless and give them a chance to have their say. Too much of American journalism really doesn't pursue the voiceless, the silenced, or the victimized.

In what ways does my vision encourage me to use my influence and power to provide both direct assistance to the poor and marginalized and to assume a position of advocacy on behalf of the voiceless and powerless?

Relieving Suffering

Peter echoes the recommendations of Colman. He counsels leaders not only to assume an advocacy role for the poor, but also to become directly involved, like Jesus, in relieving the suffering of the poor. He shares an example of how religious leaders influenced some of his direct involvement with the poor. He mentions belonging to two groups which discussed the Pastoral letter of the National Conference of Catholic Bishops, Economic Justice for All. One of the questions it raised for him and the others in the group was, "Do people really have a right to decent housing and a decent place to live?" As a result of grappling with this question, they made a decision to start a nonprofit housing corporation. From the initial purchase of a house they have grown into a sizable organization that provides fair, affordable housing to thousands of people.

Jim speaks from the credible position of living what he proclaims. He offers some advice for church leaders:

> The organized church should be more into social ministries: feeding the poor, housing the homeless. I don't sense a lot of that. But then I catch myself coming the other way and saying, "Well, who the hell is the church? The church is really the people."

The ambivalence in Jim's remarks is an outgrowth of his uncertainty regarding what he really wants and expects from church leaders. His concern is whether he really believes they should be "messing around" in areas where they have no expertise; yet he wants them to encourage Christians to develop beyond their "Sunday morning mentality." His resolution of the issue appears to lie in his hope that leaders will help people realize that "they can carry on their ministry and witness through their daily lives, whether it's called work or whatever."

How do I encourage people to organize and use their gifts to bring the gospel to bear on the problems of those who are disadvantaged? Do I challenge people to see their daily work as the crucible for their personal Christian service and ministry?

Effecting Change

Hillman, like Jim, encourages religious leaders to become personally involved in social issues and pleads with them to use their influence to encourage their people to take active roles in supporting issues which influence the quality of life for all.

> I would encourage the leadership of the congregation: "Do not compromise the word. Encourage your members to get involved in social issues because someone must make those decisions." If they don't use their influence to encourage people's involvement, perhaps an opposite set of values will deter-

mine those decisions for them. Their members will suffer, and so it is very important for them to get involved as opposed to being confined.

As a state representative, Hillman is particularly cognizant of the influence legislators have on decisions which directly affect the lives of people and the values of the community. He speaks of people's misunderstanding regarding the principle of separation of church and state. They are so fearful of any relationship between the two that they rationalize inaction and so produce a comfortable passivity regarding social issues. Hillman believes religious leaders should encourage their congregations to take direct action to influence the legislative process.

What can I do to encourage Christians to become more directly involved in the legislative process, bringing pressure to bear on legislators to enact law which creates systemic change and which is faithful to gospel values?

Opting for the Poor

Angel presents an ardent and impassioned plea for a greater commitment to the poor on the part of the church. He does not see much evidence of action to prove the existence of a "preferential option" for them.

> The church says, "Blessed are the poor," but I don't see the church going out of the way to either make the poverty more comfortable or to move people out of poverty. The church itself does not value poor people and minority people and disadvantaged people and others to the extent [that it] is willing to make very extensive changes to accommodate those people.

He expresses a fervent concern not only for the material and social needs of people, but also for the spiritual needs of people, especially poor people. Even in the midst of his extreme frustration, he saw glimmers of hope, like the example and influence of Pope John XXIII.

> I think the church is centuries behind in meeting the social needs of people and maybe very far behind in meeting the spiritual needs of people, and I think that it will take a drastic reform effort to bring it

about. About the only time I ever had any hope was
during Pope John's very brief stay in Rome in which
I felt he sincerely talked about extensive reform in
the church.

As Angel so passionately expresses, responding to the needs of
the poor requires a variety of answers. The church must deal with
both material and spiritual needs.

---

*Do I really have a "preferential option for the poor" in my vision? Do I give
more than mere lip service to that value? Have I sensitized myself not only
to the needs of the materially poor but also to the spiritually poor?*

A Multi-Faceted Response

Others also speak of the requirement for a multi-faceted
response, even suggesting there must be a broadened comprehen-
sion of who constitutes "the poor." Lee comments on how there is
often an extremely narrow concept of who constitutes the poor. She
recounts a story of a woman who might not be considered as
materially poor, but who was enveloped by a poverty of spirit.

> Someone I knew from high school showed up in my
> shop recently. I hadn't seen her in twenty years. She
> had been going through a lot of hardships. She had
> three small children and her husband was a drug
> addict. Her church saw that this woman had a need
> and arranged for her and a friend to get away for a
> weekend. I've never seen that in my church. They saw
> that she was poor in spirit, down in the dumps, and
> they helped her out. Her church helped her out finan-
> cially and spiritually. She is doing well because of the
> church's support.

---

*How does my vision have to be expanded to include a broader
understanding of who constitutes "the poor"?*

Recognizing Injustice

Lee's expanded concept of poverty is complemented by
Richard's inclusion of those who are victims of any of the "isms"

which plague our society. When discussing his role as an organizational consultant to both profit and nonprofit groups, he describes how he helps them identify and rid the workplace of these pernicious evils. He believes we need ministers who are aware of and understand unjust attitudes and behaviors. More importantly, we need ministers who are committed to eliminate them, starting with their own groups where problems exist just as they do in the workplace. Richard describes conversations he has had with ministers who know racism and sexism are present within their congregations. They justify their failure to confront this sinfulness, offering as a rationale their fear of negative reactions from parishioners.

> My message back to them is that racism and sexism
> are ageless sins that are not getting any younger and
> that we have to address them in the churches as well.
> We just can't ignore it because it's still causing per-
> sonal pain.

If the church cannot face alienating behaviors and cannot create an environment which is open and welcoming to all, how can Jesus' message of reaching all in the kingdom be promulgated? Richard speaks beyond the level of tolerance, i.e., merely giving another person his or her due. What is needed is appreciation of all that the different individuals bring, an acceptance and valuing of different gifts.

Which are the "isms" which adversely effect people in my parish or community? What are the "isms" which I must confront in the broader society? In what ways do I appreciate and celebrate the gifts of those different from me?

Raising Self-Esteem

Marge speaks along the same line as Richard, advising people in ministry that no matter how they respond to the needs of the poor, they should endeavor to do it in a way that maintains the self-esteem of the people they are attempting to help.

> I think one of the things that the folks that I work with
> need to hear is that they are valuable, that God has
> valued them, and that they're who they are, and what
> they are makes a difference. That was part of Jesus'
> message, that each of those people was valuable to
> him. Those are the people he became involved with,

that he spent his time with, and I think these folks need to realize that they are the people that Jesus would spend time with. It would be the house that they are being evicted from that Jesus would visit and spend time at.

The implication of Marge's viewpoint on the development of a vision is recognizing the need for deep human sensitivity in the way a group attempts to remedy social ills and responds to the needs of the poor. The manner in which ministry is accomplished carries important messages to the beneficiaries.

How can I sensitize myself to the fact that when I respond to the needs of the disadvantaged, I have a responsibility to do it in such a way that I maintain and strengthen their self-esteem?

Empowering Women

One group of people being victimized in our society are women. From the "feminization of poverty" to the denial of opportunity to participate fully in our organizations and institutions, over half of the population is adversely impacted by prejudice and discriminatory rules, practices, and behaviors. The negative result is obviously borne most heavily by women themselves, but the entire society suffers.

Wisdom people recommend that the church address this issue directly within itself as well as in society. It is noteworthy to realize that the people who spoke most ardently to this issue were men, especially businessmen. Arthur stated it very simply. "The church's position on women is shameful." And Mark expanded on the same theme:

I'd like to see the church address the role of women. I don't see how the institution can continue to condone a system where 50% of the world is treated in a different way than the other 50%. I think that's so fundamental. It hurts people within and without the church.

Mark praises the work of the Catholic Bishops in connection with the pastoral on the economy. Even though he does not agree with all of it, he believes that the leadership displayed by its issuance models what he expects of the bishops. At the time, he was anxiously awaiting the final version of their pastoral on women. Based on his experience in the business world, he knows the only response he can countenance is one that would challenge and denounce discrimination against women. He hopes for significant change, feeling that it is unconscionable to treat women the way he sees the church treating them today.

> [The issue of women] is an issue that, in business, we had lots of problems with twenty or thirty years ago. The biggest single problem was the basically unconscious set of beliefs that women just didn't play an active role in business. We've come a long, long way in business. Not far enough in terms of providing women with opportunities, but we've come a long way.
>
> I'm imbued with the idea that, if I'm going to learn from a teacher, I want that teacher to provide, in practice, the kind of authority that will influence me to say, "You know, that teacher lives what he says." And I'm expecting the bishops to take a very positive stand with respect to the role of women in the church. And if they don't, they are just psychologically going to lose a lot of their power, their moral power, in terms of talking to me about issues related to business, or talking to me as a citizen about issues related to peace and war and so on.
>
> The women's issue is a critical one. Fundamentally, all I am saying is, I don't know what the answers are for women in the church. I do know that they have to be dealt with openly and honestly, hopefully, in the same kind of way we try to run a business. That is to recognize everybody's dignity and to recognize the fact that, all other things being equal, we really ought to attempt to give people, men, women, white, black, what have you, the opportunity to go as far as they can and utilize their skills in the most positive and constructive way.

Although the strongest condemnation of the treatment of women in the church comes from businessmen, women clearly share similar sentiments. Pat offers her reflections and speaks about her anger at the church for its treatment of women.

They need to enfranchise women in such a way that
they have a position of respect in the formal structure
of the church, and that's got a powerful trickle down
effect. The fact that little kids and adults only see
women on the altar in positions of secondary
relationship says a lot about women and their dis-
enfranchisement as human beings. Ordain women.
Stop suppressing 51% of your organization. Let your
sexual fears and your need for power go.

I have to accept responsibility for a lot …part is I
am so angry about being disenfranchised that I
probably wouldn't recognize somebody that might
be willing to connect. I think that my feelings are true,
but the thing that I have to keep coming back to is I
am very angry about this, about the suppressed role
of women and women buying into that role. It is a
two-way street here. I feel disenfranchised in a lot of
ways.

---

*What do I need to do to sensitize myself to the issues which adversely
influence women in our church and society? How can I respond to the
injustices I see being perpetuated against women? How can I take a more
affirmative role in advocating the rights of women?*

A Prophetic Lifestyle

Ultimately, the primary mission of the church as articulated by
the wisdom people is to become a church which fosters a vision
based on the compassionate response which Jesus offered to all who
suffer, especially the poor and the disenfranchised.

Many of the interviewees long for a church which reflects the
values of the early, apostolic church, the church described in the Acts
of the Apostles. Colman views that early church primarily as a
community whose organizing principle was its members' sharing
generously all that they had and acting as advocates for peace.

Share the wealth. It's right in the Acts of the Apostles.
I love to read that document not as a matter of faith
but just as a document of sociology. How did these
rebel dissidents organize? It's always a great mystery
how people organize and advance their cause. I am

always fascinated by that. When you read the Acts of the Apostles you see that they organized around sharing their wealth. That was basic. The second thing they did was to organize around peace and nonviolence. Both of those have been lost.

The commitment to sharing one's assets is further elucidated by Anthony.

The big problem in the world today is the tremendous materialism, the division of society into the have's and have not's, and that's increasing. How can the church lead us better, move us. Not that it is only the church's role, but to keep those things before us more continuously. The ideal of giving and sharing and accepting other people and trying to help other people be what they can be. I mean the church says those things, but somehow it doesn't keep them before us as a challenge. The economic pastoral seemed like a good document and there was a lot of talk about it, but it certainly seemed to fade away like it was never there within a short period of time. I guess it is information that maybe a majority of people don't want to hear; yet, it seems to me it's the prophetic mission of the church.

Anthony continues to expound on this theme, pointing out that in the United States, we set a high ideal for what constitutes an adequate standard of living. While this is so, he notes that poor countries have implicitly set a higher standard for charity than we have. Our values as a society, therefore, seem more narcissistic and self-serving than generous and other-centered. He recommends that religious leaders challenge people against the impulse to be overly-acquisitive and materialistic.

Anthony goes on in this vein, speculating that, "comfortable, middle class, middle life and later life people" seem to set a priority that "the highest virtue is total security." If people observe "comfortable, middle class" ministers modeling a life of security and acquisitiveness, it will be impossible for them to challenge their congregations to imitate the early Christians "who shared all things in common."

Does my vision challenge people to evaluate their responsibility to share their gift of wealth with others who are deprived of the very necessities of life? As a Christian leader, what witness do I give to people through the lifestyle I live?

Peacemaking

The final component for the vision is that provided by Colman: that the church be known as a peacemaking church.

> Ghandi was right when he said the only people on earth who don't understand that Christianity is a religion of nonviolence are the Christians. It's amazing. Here you have a religion that was established by a rabbi and a group of dissident rebels founded on absolute nonviolence. There were absolutes: love your enemies, do good to those who hurt you, share your wealth, and no violence. It couldn't be clearer. Nobody has a higher calling than to be a peacemaker, to make it easier for people to be good not a peace seeker or a peace lover but a peacemaker. And all of us have to figure out and examine our consciences to determine exactly what we can do to create conditions in our personal lives and in our collective political lives to make it easier for people to be good. We ought to be known as a peace church.

Where do I have to take initiatives to foster peace, forgiveness, and reconciliation in my personal and communal life?

Conclusion

To the wisdom people the vision is clear: live as Jesus did and embrace the words of the gospel as the only criteria for action. Their suggestions for what should constitute the vision for the church broadly and for individual groups are not all-inclusive. They are presented to stimulate reflection on what it is that should shape the vision for any church organization.

One further point regarding vision: the visions developed for sub-groups should be linked to that for the overall organization. For example, the local parish might embrace a strong, socially-responsible, outwardly-focused vision. It is then an imperative for all the groups within the parish to be similarly directed. The parish vision will not be achieved if individual groups establish and follow visions not aligned with that of the parish.

We suggest that the questions included in this chapter provide an ideal instrument for reflection and discussion by leaders and, especially, leadership groups. This will help build a context for listening. It will allow the group to learn from personal visions what might be the shared vision for the entire organization. It will provide the leader the opportunity to challenge assumptions, question paradigms, and bring to the group an in-depth understanding of gospel values which should inform any vision which is developed.

6
Ministry: An Expanded Concept of Leadership

> All I've ever wanted to do was to be a mother and a
> hairdresser, so that must be my ministry.
>
> Lee

In spite of the many pronouncements about the role of the laity in the world, there seems to be within the church a very restrictive view of what constitutes ministry. All too often, ministry is seen as activities which are sanctioned by the church, are formally set up through the agency of the church, or are led by people appointed by the church. Ministries are defined within local parishes, for example, as the functioning committees which address everything from social justice issues to property maintenance. This is ministry, but to define it only in terms of such church-related activities is to miss most of the opportunities for extending the kingdom of God.

With the increase in the number of women working full-time outside the home and with all Americans spending more time on the job than did their parents, they have few hours available to devote to formal church ministries. We believe that the church documents alluded to above hold the answer: that the work people do day-to-day should be considered their ministry. For the church to be effective in achieving a gospel-bound, mission-focused vision, a leadership which understands a broadened concept of ministry and behaves accordingly is needed.

The authors share a deep concern about ministry, both ecclesial ministry and that ministry carried out in people's day-to-day lives, especially in the marketplace. As we undertook our research project, we wanted to know how people see their work in relationship to the concept of "ministry." Some acquaintances advised against even asking such a question, suggesting that the term "ministry" would be a turn-off for most people. We tested it, however, and decided to retain the question, asking people if they view what they are doing in the marketplace as ministry. The response was almost universal; their work is indeed their ministry, some even describing it as their call. A number said that they made a definite choice to continue in their present occupation because they view it as ministry. Others went so far as to equate their occupation with their "mission." Interestingly, while these people are clear in their understanding of what they do as ministry and value it in those terms, their most compelling remarks indicate that they are doubtful their pastors and other church leaders share this conviction. They never hear their work so characterized.

What is the gap between formal church pronouncements about the role of laity and their church experience as they interact with religious leaders?

Ministry as Described by the Wisdom People

Too often definitions limit our understanding and appreciation of the things defined. We hope that the insights provided by the wisdom people will expand leaders' thinking, stimulating a reevaluation of their own concepts of ministry, and ultimately removing an impediment to leadership effectiveness.

Lee's conversation, quoted at the beginning of this chapter, tells the story of her awakening to the fact that her ministry is as compelling and powerful as any which is carried out under the direct auspices of the church.

Lee was the only person in the group interviewed who was recommended by two different people. Those who nominated her claimed that when visiting Lee to have their hair done, they felt ministered to. Yet, when asked if she saw what she was doing as ministry, she hesitated. She suggested that prior to being invited into the interview, she had viewed ministry as "something done in the church." She would not, therefore, have conceived of herself as a minister. As she prepared for the interview, however, she thought about what she does in a different way, triggered by the fact that those who nominated her saw her work in larger terms than she herself did. Her reflection led her to realize that she is ministering, she is a minister. It was from this thought process that she now describes ministry as, "Touching other people's lives in a positive way." When we asked if her pastor would see what she is doing as ministry, Lee replied, "Probably not." Clearly, his definition of ministry is a limited one, one which he and others apparently passed on to Lee. She had never before been challenged to think of what she does as ministry.

Interestingly, soon after our interview with Lee, we had the opportunity to conduct a clergy education program in the diocese where she lives. Sharing her story, including her perception of what her pastor's response would typically be, we added that he might be among those attending. Lee later reported that the Sunday after the clergy education conference, her pastor preached on the value of the ministry of Christians in the workplace!

After Lee's initial reticence in the interview, she became quite eloquent about her emerging understanding of ministry. It was an exhilarating experience to feel her excitement as she dealt with her new insights. She had an enhanced sense of self-esteem and power, a feeling that she might do even more, buoyed by the confidence in her that others had expressed. Her new understanding of ministry truly came as a gift from those who nominated her. She can now appreciate herself as a minister. She better understands where her ministry lies, seeing herself as most effective when addressing the needs of her women clients. She helps them feel better about themselves, not in a narcissistic way, but healthily appreciating and valuing themselves.

Lee also mentions that she ministers to the families of recently deceased people through the care she takes in arranging the hair of the deceased at a local mortuary. Her compassion is evident as she reflects on the pain that the families are experiencing and how her ministry is a consolation to them. Her witness is using her professional skills to live out a corporal work of mercy.

Lee concludes her reflections on ministry with her remark about being both a mother and a hairdresser. Then, and with a broad smile, she adds two additional roles: "a friend and a psychologist" to those she serves.

Like Lee's astute definition of ministry as a way of touching people's lives, other wisdom people provide similarly profound insights to challenge some common and narrow definitions of ministry, presenting a more expansive concept of what ministry involves.

Dawne expands on the idea of ministry as something encompassing one's entire life, describing how she came to realize the breadth of ministry in her work:

> The paperwork at first was something I felt was a job. Gradually, I have begun to see that the letters I write are also an opportunity to minister. The words that I choose, the tone of the letter, the promptness of it, not keeping people waiting, giving them what they want or need in whatever form that might take is ministry.

Clearly, Dawne can see in the subtleties of all she does how ministry is fostered in how she reaches and impacts others.

Ministry is touching people in profoundly Christian ways in all that we do. Ministry may be implicit in the manner in which one extends himself or herself to another, as in the way Lee supports her customers, listening to their pain and comforting them. Or it may be explicit, with the minister specifically seeking people out and letting them know that she or he is there to minister. Examples of this would be showing a willingness to discuss troublesome ethical issues or calling a group to its broader social responsibilities as it makes business decisions.

Nancy acknowledges that what she does daily at the office is truly ministry, which she describes as an attitude and an approach, rather than a specific occupation:

> I think all life is a ministry and you are called to do whatever you are doing. Ministry is a way of doing something, rather than a particular occupational role.

Serving as a lawyer for congress, she drafts legislation which will have positive social impact. She knows the law intimately and speaks with animation and glee as she describes her role in assisting a native American tribe to successfully litigate a claim. Her work is so important to her that she says:

> Even if I knew I was going to die two months from now or a year from now, I would definitely continue in this job, because it is meaningful and important. With my background and skills and interests, it's the best thing I could be doing right now. I feel that this is a job where I can really be of service to the public. I can really think in terms of what really makes the

most sense from an overall policy perspective …just
being able to take a larger, social approach…

Joe shares the insight which came to him when he attended a
business vocations conference. His ministerial awakening occurred
as he listened to one of the speakers. What struck him was the
realization that through his position at work he has the opportunity
to influence the lives and behaviors of people in a most forceful and
meaningful way:

> Up to that point, I never thought of my work as a
> ministry. The lights went on and now I see it as a
> ministry. It's not that I'm doing anything differently,
> but I am seeing it as a ministry.

Joe becomes lively as he describes his excitement in being able
to have a positive influence on the development and growth of
employees throughout the organization. The thing that is most evident about this man is the enthusiasm he has for his work, his
ministry:

> I really enjoy working. I like my people. I like the
> environment. I like impacting, making things hap-
> pen. I like hiring people. I like seeing people grow.

While Joe's awareness was sudden, triggered by the conference
speaker he heard, others come to an appreciation of their career as
ministry in more gradual ways. Caroline had been a Catholic school
principal for eight years before she realized in a full sense that she
had a vocation, a calling, a ministry. She describes how a "simple
little booklet" about the role of the principal provided the stimulus
for her reflection, leading her to new, exciting, and energizing insights about what she is doing. She relates how she "imaged" her
role, ceasing to look at it as merely a job, and seeing it as something
to which the Lord calls her. She now views it as "a vocation."

For Sharon, it was a traumatic incident which enabled her to
develop an understanding of how her role as a personnel director is
her ministry. The catalyst for her was the devastating impact that
layoffs in her company were having, not only on the people who lost
their jobs, but on the entire organization. Recalling the varied responses of people to the crisis of losing their jobs, she came to realize the
importance of her own role. "I had never experienced such a
profound sense of ministry as I had on that day." She is grateful for
the support that she receives from others in her field who have faced

similar challenges. She especially praised one person employed as a human resource specialist in a hospital who often gives her a reinforcing message, "You know, this is our ministry."

Peter differentiates between what he sees as ministry with a capital "M" and ministry with a small "m". "I see what I do in the workplace as a small "m" meaning just being of service to others, trying to serve others and giving something back." In Peter's statement there is, perhaps, the key to the difficulty that some leaders have with ministry; they see only capital "M" ministry as valid, that done under the specific auspices of the church, neither recognizing nor supporting that which is carried out by people each day.

Jim, who heads a construction company, tells of his struggles with making daily decisions which are complicated by tensions between the pressures and practices of the industry and his personal life as a Christian. He talks about the pain he felt as he attempted to deal with day to day decisions, going so far as to seek counseling to bring some of his conflicts to resolution. The result was that he came to a new and creative awareness: "I've got to make my job my ministry." He saw the need to be true to himself, to live by his values of compassion and fairness, if he was going to be at peace with himself and still run a successful company. When we pressed Jim to define what makes what he is doing in the construction business a ministry, he identified a number of elements:

> We really believe that what we do is to serve God. We have an obligation to everyone who works here to take care of them. We have an obligation to take care of our subcontractors ... to be fair with people ... to set a good example. It's like putting yourself in their place and knowing their hurts and their troubles. They have to make a living and they have families to support.

Ministry as a Call

Traditionally in the church we have referred to a vocation as a "call." Like Lee who is clear that her call and ministry are to be a mother and hairdresser, others also use the term "call" to express their conviction that what they do daily in the marketplace is their ministry.

Elizabeth describes the nurses in her unit as consciously identifying what they do, not only as a ministry, but as a calling. Like Lee, ministry for Elizabeth and her co-workers is touching other people. But the touching is special; it is not merely physical care, it is reaching deeper. "We touch people at the core of their being."

Scott expands on this concept:

> Organizing is not a career and not a profession: it's a vocation. You really feel called to do it. I don't know where that comes from and I don't know why I feel like that. If I'm not doing this, I'm not doing what I'm supposed to be doing. In my case it's so clear…I have a call.

Marge describes the evolution of her understanding of her work as a call. Her major ministry is working in a school with children and their families.

> When I first went into this work, I saw it as a job I'd be involved in for awhile, and then maybe I'd get into more formal church ministry. There's a sense of reality [to] what I'm doing there that's so powerful. You can be such an agent of change in that situation. It's just incredible.

When asked what she means by being a change agent, Marge responds, "What you are, even more than what you do, has an impact on people in the workplace." She gives a number of poignant examples of "little throw away things" which carry strong messages to others, illustrating the fact that living one's values consistently ultimately has a strong influence on people. Marge's one caution is that a person must always be alert to "discern that I'm being called to do something in this situation to impact people." Self-awareness, not self-consciousness, is needed to know how best to serve and to convey to others the strength of one's values. For Marge, her gift is "standing with people," being present to them. From her experience she encourages church leaders to stress with people how significant each one is. It is through one's individuality and gifts that a person makes a difference in the lives of others. Such affirmation helps people to discern their call and enhances the value of their ministry.

Christians With a Mission

Many equate their careers with ministry. Some go even further, referring to what they do in the marketplace as their "mission." This view was not restricted to those who are in the traditional helping professions. It cut across the entire spectrum of occupations.

Richard had been the victim of racial prejudice and bias. It is out of this reality that he describes "my mission to help others and myself to continue to grow and learn." He uses the painful as the vehicle for transformation to the good, not allowing bitterness and cynicism to gain ascendancy.

Mirta who, like Richard, is a member of an ethnic minority, describes her mission in terms of "co-creation." She is an enabler. As she has learned to grow through life experience, she helps others to free themselves to be themselves.

A strong sense of mission infuses Chris's view of his dual role as manager and publisher:

> I see what I do here with my employees as my ministry and my mission. That's important. In a sense, you accept responsibility for people when you accept a management role. I see the mission in what I do. I really believe that the gospel message of love in this crazy world is the only solution to the problems we face, and in some small way, I think here, through our publishing, we can bring [out] the gospel values, reinterpreting those values and making the gospel relevant in the contemporary world.

Chris believes this so strongly that he decided to stay with his present company even though it meant foregoing an opportunity for financial and professional advancement. He was not convinced he could do the things he believes are important in publishing had he gone with another company.

As is evident from these examples, the wisdom people are clear in their understanding of ministry: it extends far beyond their church-related activities and flowers primarily where they live their daily workplace lives. Their view is not novel or radical. It is consistent with the long-established teaching of the churches, restated by the Second Vatican Council in the 1960s and by the recent Synod on the Laity, held in Rome in 1987.

> All the baptized participate in the mission in the world, the church's secular vocation, but do so in different ways. For lay Christians their presence and activity in the world is not something simply incidental; rather it is central to their vocation; the "world"

is the environment and the means by which a lay
Christian lives out his or her vocation.

The Church and an Expanded Concept of Ministry

One of the sad lessons learned from this research is the gap
alluded to earlier. On the one hand, we have the clear, powerful, and
forthright documents issued by the institutional churches, stressing
the validity and value of the ministries of laity in the marketplace.
On the other, there appears to be very little acknowledgement,
affirmation, and support of that concept by many church leaders. All
too often their bias—and we speak of church teachers, pastoral
council members, religious education directors, pastoral ministers,
clergy, and religious—is to favor church-sponsored ministry, failing
to recognize that many people do not have the interest, skills, or time
for such ministry. People are heavily challenged by what they do
daily and would dilute their effectiveness were they to take on
additional ministry-work. Interestingly, while people see no higher
value in church-sponsored ministry (merely because it is church-
sponsored) than what they are doing, many in church leadership do
differentiate, stressing the significance of church-sponsored ministry
over that performed in the world of work.

This is not the viewpoint taken by Bishop Howard Hubbard of
the Diocese of Albany. In a recent pastoral letter, he asserts that the
preeminent ministry is ministry in the world. All other is in support
of that: the liturgical, sacramental and educational ministries of the
church exist to prepare people to assume their ministry in the world.

The thinking of Hubbard is not new. It was Archbishop Ireland,
one of the first Catholic archbishops in the United States who stated:

> We are certain of failure if we are in the sanctuary
> when we should be in the highways and byways. If
> we are on our knees, when we should be fleet of foot.

For many the criterion of sanctity was the amount of time one
spent in private prayer. Ireland challenges that assumption, maintaining that true Christianity and true spirituality are social in nature,
exemplified in compassionate action and not sedentary piety.

The Synod on the Laity produced many statements supporting
and encouraging the ministry of the laity in the marketplace. Perhaps
no one captured it as well as Cardinal O'Feigh, the Primate of Ireland,
who stood in the midst of that august assembly and declared:

> Patty O'Shea was a man who went to church;
> He never missed a Sunday,
> But when he died, he went to hell
> For what he did on Monday.

At the same synod, Archbishop Worlock of Liverpool declared:

> More people, priests, religious and laity, share in the
> life of the church than ever before. But I have to ask
> myself the extent to which the renewal of the secular
> order has been a primary concern within the church.
> Have the laity turned away from their vocation in the
> world and from public life and politics because they
> have not wished to be contaminated by the corruption
> of the "affairs of the world?" Or has there been so much
> concentration on the renewal of worship and struc-
> tures of the church that lay persons have been drawn
> into new ministries and structures of dialogue and
> perhaps overlooked their secular responsibilities?

Monsignor Peter Coughlan, then Undersecretary of the Pontifi-
cal Council for the Laity, sums up one of the major points of that
synod:

> Today, in the world of economy and work, transfor-
> mations are taking place which are a cause for serious
> concern. The lay faithful should be in the front line in
> working out solutions to the extremely serious
> problems of growing unemployment. They must
> fight to overcome in a timely way the numerous
> injustices that arise from unacceptable ways of or-
> ganizing work. They must strive to make the
> workplace a community of persons who are
> respected in their uniqueness and in their right to
> participation: They must arouse new forms of
> entrepreneurship and review the systems of com-
> merce, finance, and the exchange of technology.

Lest you think these are recent concepts in the American church,
we offer the insights of Archbishop Spalding who in 1902 com-
plained that the denial of apostolic opportunities to the laity does
not flow from the nature of the church. Rather, "those who happen
to share her course and policy at the moment are narrow and
unintelligent."

With such clear documents illuminating the expansive concept of ministry, it is disheartening to realize that those engaged in ministries in the world are not often acknowledged by church leaders. What we heard from the wisdom people is that there is little encouragement and support extended to those laboring in the world. There are few homilies which deal substantively with the issues they regularly face. Adult education programs that they might attend are mostly focused on church-related themes. Their occupations and skills are recognized and supported only when some value from them might accrue to the church organization. The wisdom people tell us that rarely is their responsibility for carrying Jesus' message to the world proclaimed, explored, and celebrated.

We believe that one of the roots of the problem is a limited view of spirituality on the part of church leaders. Rather than seeing full integration of all that one is and does as the substance of the spiritual life, they emphasize the explicitly spiritual activities with which they are primarily concerned. Sadly, the result is that many people find leaders' messages somewhat irrelevant. What they emphasize does not deal with the realities of daily life where spiritual concepts and values are tested. Just as we want legislators to incorporate Christian values into the laws they write to recall the point that Hillman makes we want to see church leaders who understand the challenges their people face as they attempt to live out their Christian values and beliefs.

Conclusion

Reflection on the insights of the wisdom people and the pronouncements of church commentators quoted above might assist Christian leaders in evaluating their own understanding of ministry. We suggest that all Christian leaders enter into dialogue and *listen* to people like those we have introduced. They have much to say and much valuable information to impart. They need support and can become even more effective in their ministries if leaders are willing to invest time and energy.

The benefits which accrue to leaders and to the community from support of workplace ministries of the laity are significant:
- The influence of the church in promulgating Christian values is greatly extended.
- The workplace serves as the crucible in which the strength of homiletic messages can be tested.

- Support of laity is empowering, conveying their vital role as co-disciples in bringing the kingdom of God to reality.
- Recognizing the gifts of the laity builds a stronger sense of community.
- The involvement of laity in such ministry provides the church with ears to hear the needs of the broader community.

Reflection Questions

1. How do I define ministry?

2. Is this definition of ministry broad or narrow?

3. In what ways does my church organization/group support the ministries of people in the world?

4. In my organization/group, does ministry with a capital "M" takes precedence over that with a lower case "m"?

7

Collaboration:
The How of Leadership

I personally put a great deal of importance on a sense of
community, on belonging to a community.

Chris

Someone recently said flippantly, "The lone minister will quickly
become the lonely minister." If leaders believe that they can manage
autocratically, they will find their support eroding. While some
faithful members may hang on, little fresh blood will flow in to help
the group grow and flourish. Simply stated, leaders who attempt to
minister in isolation from their people will be ineffective in today's
church. We are convinced that collaborative leadership is what our
times demand. Fortunately, Christian leaders have an ideal collaborative model in Jesus.

When comparing Jesus to other leaders, the striking thing is that
Jesus is nearly always surrounded by his followers. The apostles and
disciples are with him, talking, asking questions, helping people in
the gathering, witnessing what Jesus stood for, and, ultimately,
following the model he created. The image of Jesus presented in the
scriptures is one of a leader in constant relationship and dialogue
with his followers. From the very beginning of his ministry, Jesus
chose to lead with others. He gathered people around him, invited
them to join him, listened patiently to them, taught them new ways
of approaching things, and empowered them to carry on with others.
Clearly, Jesus did not minister in isolation from his community. The
denial of Peter illustrates the importance of the group in Jesus'
approach to leadership. The incident is all the more powerful because not only did Peter deny Jesus, he also denied being "one of

them," the followers of Jesus. Peter was rejecting his community as well as his leader. This is in direct contrast to the charge that Jesus gives to his disciples: that they go out "two by two," not alone, to minister. He affirms them in their giftedness, receives them back when they return from ministry, and helps them reflect on and learn from their experiences. Ultimately, Jesus leaves them, believing in their ability and power to carry on without him because they have the Spirit to guide them. This is indeed a powerful model for any faith-based collaborative leader.

A Paradigm for Collaborative Ministry

William Borders, the retired Catholic Archbishop of Baltimore, wrote a challenging pastoral letter on ministry called *We Are His People*. It clearly identifies what collaboration involves for contemporary Christian leaders. Borders' overall framework is that the church is "a community of collaborative ministry." He says that the process for the leader who wishes to develop a collaborative community involves three major tasks:

1. to help each member see his or her baptism as a call to holiness and ministry;
2. to assist all members to discern and discover their personal gifts and charisms so that they might be used in ministry and service;
3. to see the leader's primary role and responsibility as fostering participation of all the People of God in the mission of the church.

Borders' paradigm is a strong ideal for Christian leaders because it emphasizes the preeminence of gifts as the foundation for collaborative ministry. It also stresses the role of the leader in developing and utilizing gifts found throughout the community. This is a model faithful to that which Jesus practiced. The theological foundation for collaborative ministry is clear in the scriptures. Not only does Jesus work in this way, the Acts of the Apostles reveal a group working together to develop the young Christian church. A critical decision made very early with the Jew-Gentile debate was that the church be inclusive rather than exclusive. Paul complements Acts with his letters, some of the most memorable of which deal with gifts and how they are dispersed through the community.

Unfortunately, pastoral practice often lags behind theology. There is hope, however, in the phrase of a friend who proclaimed with a touch of cynicism, "Necessity is the mother of theology!" With this in mind, if theological and scriptural foundations for leaders' adopting a collaborative approach are not convincing, practicality makes collaboration a compelling choice. The pragmatic reality is the need to involve more people in ministry if burn-out and over-extension are to be avoided.

The Development of Collaboration Within the Business World

For a variety of historical and practical reasons, hierarchical models of leadership were developed and persist today in most of our institutions. But there are significant changes in process. Within the Catholic church, the shift came with the Second Vatican Council and its emphasis on church as the "People of God." In the world of business, dramatic changes in organizational structures and inter-personal relationships are bringing about rapid transformation. The following are illustrations of the kind of change going on in business:

- emphasis on distributed power, enabling people closest to the customer to take action without checking with the boss;
- teams composed of people with different levels of responsibility who often have no supervisory-subordinate relationship;
- self-directed units in which workers have the ability to plan their work, assess their performance, and hire new people;
- supervisory candidates interviewed and selected by the people whom they will supervise;
- major companies forming strategic alliances with other corporations to gain access to markets, new technology, or to reduce individual risk.

The world of work and the organizations which drive it are obviously undergoing radical change. Partnerships, teams, alliances, and linkages are the language of the day, but the primary emphasis is on responsible individuals working cooperatively with others to achieve agreed-upon goals.

What is most significant for our purposes as we talk about leadership within the church is that people in the work-world are experiencing new forms of leadership and organization. The leader is no longer the expert, but the team leader. His or her title is often changed to "support manager" or "coach" and the role becomes one of helping and facilitating. Workers are taking on more responsibility, are dealing with each other as peers rather than as competitors, are expected to assume a leadership point of view as they perform their tasks, and are hopefully finding greater personal fulfillment through their involvement in the total process.

Ted, who runs an organization of hundreds of highly-trained professional people doing technical analysis, speaks about the difficulty some people have with teamwork:

> I've had discussions with my people because teamwork is a very important word in [this organization]. I have one group [made up of people] in the top two to five percent of their university classes. I said to them, "Everyone of you, you've been competitive since you were a little kid, through high school, getting into the top colleges. Now, after twenty-three years of that, I'm telling you that two weeks after coming in here, you have to be a team player. That's going to be tough for you, but that's what we're asking you to do.

Ted realizes that teamwork must be a value in his organization if the group is to achieve its highly complex tasks. He sees his role as one of coach, to help those who have difficulty with the team approach learn how to work with others and be noncompetitive within the group.

What does this example of how people in the workplace are expected to operate suggest about their expectations of leaders in other places especially in the church which professes to be a community?

Effective collaborative leaders focus on the development of team and community. As Joel Baker comments, "The team approach will be the hallmark of the great companies of the twenty-first century." This does not suggest that leaders will no longer be needed, rather that the leadership role is significantly altered. It is much less "top down" and much more a "with you" or "I support you" approach. One of the most interesting forms of leadership to emerge in the business world in the last few decades is that of "servant leadership." Even the term itself conjures up the essence of Christian leadership if we think of the empowering message Jesus conveyed by washing the apostles' feet. Servant leadership involves:

> Increased service to others, taking a more holistic approach to work, promoting a sense of community

within an organization and the greater community, sharing of power and decision making, and a group-oriented approach to work in contrast to the hierarchical model.

Clearly, the expectations placed on leaders are changing. Our belief is that the team or collaborative model will be the hallmark of effective, mission-oriented churches of the twenty-first century.

The Wisdom People and Collaboration

One of the reasons why the wisdom people are effective in their marketplace leadership is because of their emphasis on being collaborative. This is their *modus operandi*. They see value for both their ministry and themselves in working with others, rather than working in isolation.

The development of community or team is the preferred leadership style of the wisdom people. Not a single person in the interview group reveals a radically individualistic approach. These are people who see community as more than a value. It is an absolute need, something integral to effectively carry out their daily activities, to perform Christian ministry and service. Based on their own experience, they encourage Christian leaders to develop more collaborative and communal structures and behaviors.

As we listen to the words of the wisdom people, we find that their view of collaboration is rooted deeply in a sense of community. Several speak in terms of church as family, as a unit working together to support each other and common goals. As leaders carrying varying levels of authority and responsibility, they offer a model which others can use to assess their commitment to community, shared responsibility, and power. The rationale for fostering collaboration and community ranges from realizing that their absence is contradictory to what Christianity is about to the awareness that it is simply more enjoyable to work and minister with others.

Grace states the need for collaboration quite bluntly, "I think that individualism kills Christ's spirit. It doesn't build the spirit that needs to be there." The difficulty is that individualism is like a performance, pleasing some and displeasing others. It can be inspiring to one group while it leaves others feeling distant and unconnected. Working collaboratively helps to clarify the motivation for the action; the involvement of many builds and expands the spirit for the whole.

Lee, who identifies her ministry as being both mother and hairdresser, describes how she intentionally attempts to build community among her clients.

> For the women who come to my shop, it is a social event. It's almost like a little community. The people minister to each other while they are waiting. They have a lot in common. They didn't know each other before they came, [but] they become a little group of friends. I try to connect people with each other.

Scott, with his dedication to the poor, says that working together not only builds power to effect change, "It's also fun." While not many of the wisdom people identify the issue as "fun," it is evident that they are generally joyful, life-filled people, relishing their involvement with others. In contrast, leaders who labor in isolation are prone to see the world from a limited vantage point, lack adequate feedback to challenge and animate them, and may suffer loneliness and depression.

The Emphasis on Community

For many of the wisdom people community is a value because people know that their effectiveness is enhanced by functioning as a team member. It provides opportunities for them to learn from the viewpoints and skills within the group. Others reflect that the spirit of community empowers them to be more enthusiastic and zealous in their undertakings. Regardless of their professions—educators, hairdressers, doctors, executives—the wisdom people talk of needing and valuing community.

Heading a highly-specialized medical team, Frat reflects:

> I realized that if we are going to change these patients, if we are going to have them leave the unit with a sense of dignity and sense of self-esteem, I can't do that by myself. I have to have the prayer and support from other people outside, but I also have to have a team that is focused on the same goals...the same value system.

There are two compelling issues in Frat's statement. First, the team is larger than simply those in the operating room; it includes "people outside" who offer prayer and are spiritually committed. Second, there is no question that Frat, as the physician, heads the team. A common set of goals and values is essential for everyone on the team to help restore the patient's health.

Talking about his attempt to live his Christian values, Peter stresses the need to bond with others of like values so that when one person is "up" and another "down," the ministry can continue. Community in this sense is a kind of insurance policy for both team effectiveness and the well-being of the individual member:

> I can't do [things] alone. I need the reinforcement the witnessing of others. You might be on a downweek, but someone else is on an upweek. Through the sharing comes encouragement. I really find it is very difficult to try to live out a ministry by yourself. It's really important for me to have a sense of community.

Community as an Extension of Family

Chris, quoted at the beginning of this chapter, states the significant value of community in his own life and shares how he was influenced by an awareness gained in college. "Community was something they always talked about, a sense of family." That message has had a positive influence on his attitude toward the people who work with and for him:

> I think it's very important for people to work for something larger than themselves, and I get that here. There's a lot of joy and a lot of pride in that. You feel a part of something larger. We're all striving for a common goal. That's important to me and becomes more and more important as I get older.

Chris's equating community with family is a theme echoed by others. It appears implicitly in the words of Irene and Randy who operate two successful restaurants and whose concerns for their staff extend well beyond the service provided to those coming to eat.

> So we have always been, if anything, held back to an extent by not trying to be wealthy, and get back into refocusing on what we have and then sharing. You know we have [shared] for so many years with our employees. We have tried to make a good life for them taking the time to try to help them through many difficulties, trying to get them to realize what values we have and share, trying to get them to

> realize that they need to try to build on whatever
> small start they may have. Because it is only through
> a sense of accomplishment that you can really build.

This is a holistic view of collaboration. Irene and Randy's concern for their employees is truly "family" because it extends beyond the eight-hour day. They speak movingly of an alcoholic who overcame her addiction and of another whom they lost to it. They are deeply involved in their employees' lives. Yet, their vehicle for building their team is the work. It is to have everyone understand how all they do is focused on pleasing their customers. This is not driven solely by a profit motive; it is driven by their deeply-held value that their staff will feel good about themselves and build their self-esteem by extending service and themselves personally to others.

The metaphor of family provides a rich insight into collaborative ministry. There is differentiation of roles; there is mutual sharing; there is support of each other, especially in times of stress and challenge. Most importantly for the Christian community, love is the foundation for the family relationship. Clearly, the metaphor also carries some negative connotations which can serve as caution signs for collaboration: too strong a maternal or paternal role, sibling rivalry, and creating scapegoats. Leaders who have had positive experiences of family often draw on some of its more generative aspects to strengthen their collaborative ministry. As a result, they develop a ministerial climate which attracts and nourishes people because it relates to what so many are comfortable with from their own experience.

The Faith Community

A further dimension of community which some of the wisdom people discuss is the value and need for faith-sharing. They are convinced that being part of a supportive faith community empowers them to live their Christian vocation to the fullest. Kaylujan ties several of these themes together:

> I like to come here to church because this is my family.
> For church *is* an extended family. I just have to come
> to church. I need church because of the stress that I'm
> under the rest of the time. The church doesn't need
> me. I need the church. It's an extended family for me.

The interesting paradox of Kaylujan's experience of church as family is her saying it is she who needs the church, not vice versa. Indeed, the church does need her and obviously is creating an environment which is welcoming to her.

Marge, a speech pathologist, shares the strong sense of support she feels from the other teachers with whom she works because of the common values they share. She describes the faculty as a community, recounting a story of how they worked together to find housing for one of their students and his mother who had been displaced from their home.

Marge comments that people often tell her that they see qualities in her that they would like to emulate. They are curious as to the source of her personal strength and how they might develop their own. She tries to convey the importance of having community support as she attempts to live her values. She urges them to seek out "a strong community of faith," one in which people are willing to witness their mutual dependency and a sense of unity. If that spirit is lacking, those they hope to reach will turn elsewhere.

Caroline, a principal, speaks of her goal for the parochial school she heads: to develop a strong faith community to provide support and witness to the people whom they are trying to serve the children, their families, members of the parish, and the broader community. She is convinced that the school will be effective in carrying out its goal of Christian education only if all associated with it, especially faculty and staff, model and witness what they believe. Psychologist Abraham Maslow claims that if people are to grow, they need two things, models and challenge. Caroline realizes that if the faculty and staff, as Christian leaders do not work through the difficulties of building community and reveal its benefits, it is impossible to call others to live Christian community.

A few years ago we worked with a faculty. The receptionist at the school, a teen-age girl who knew we were there to conduct the program asked, "How come the faculty keeps talking about the value of community and challenging us to work at building community, yet they don't even talk with each other?" Behaviors reveal the value structure of any group, not the words they might include in their mission and vision statements. Caroline works hard to prevent a gap between what is said and what is done in her school, realizing that her team will be successful building a faith community to the extent that they function as a faith community.

Mutual Dialogue and Decision-Making

While modeling is the first task of collaborative leaders, they must also develop opportunities for mutual dialogue and shared decision-making. Lack of these may create an atmosphere of suspicion, hostility, and competition, rather than one of collaboration.

Mark has had a number of opportunities to speak on the topic of the Christian vocation of a business leader. He includes in his remarks the need to create opportunities for laity and clergy to come together for mutual dialogue, believing that only when this occurs will we be able to discard the caricatures which inevitably arise on both sides and prevent us from valuing each other. The result of dialogue is that people become comfortable speaking from their person, not from their designated roles. They grow in appreciation and acceptance of each other.

It was through news coverage of a hostage situation that we learned a strategy used by negotiators faced with seemingly irreconcilable differences between two parties. They attempt to force both captors and hostages into very close quarters, knowing that when antagonists are physically close to each other, they are more likely to communicate in a more personal way. The more they get to know each other, the more likely they are to understand each other's expectations and start moving to resolution.

There is relevant wisdom to be learned from this strategy. When laity and their leaders dialogue and encounter the humanness and vulnerability of each other, they are more likely to appreciate each other's uniqueness and goodness, even if they disagree in viewpoint. Dialogue creates the atmosphere which enhances the potential for more effective collaboration in a common mission.

Joe recommends a specific area in which communication and dialogue can lead to better collaboration: opening explicit lines of communication between the church leaders and the business community. He believes that such dialogue can lead "to a greater degree of respect for what each other does and can do." Such dialogue will allow leaders to see opportunities for ministry in the world. Additionally, the business experience of laity is a valued resource they can provide to help the church in its mission effectiveness. Joe's viewpoint was a recurrent one in our interviews. Many church leaders are less than receptive to this available expertise and are, in fact, often threatened by it. People spoke of offering to help, only to be refused or ignored. They leave the encounter angry, sensing they are under-valued. They also become critical, seeing decisions made and actions taken that do not make sense from a professional standpoint.

Unless communication and dialogue move beyond the mutual respect stage to the point of shared decision-making, many people will ultimately feel alienated. This involves more than just business-based issues. Pat identifies a number of areas where she believes the wisdom of the laity would be most beneficial in decision-making.

> Consider alternate ways of solving problems: let people become more active in the church instead of just figureheads. Involve them in making decisions about the church as a community. There are some real big issues that confront couples and individuals today. For example, in rethinking the whole idea of birth control. It's archaic. I mean nobody is dealing with the responsibility of over-populating this one earth that we have. We need to rethink that. And rethinking this idea of divorce. There needs to be input from educational and professional people that are qualified.

Part of the dialogue, perhaps the most difficult part, for many people in church leadership is to listen to the complaints, the frustrations, and the perceived failures which discourage people from committing themselves more fully to the church and its mission. It is difficult to listen to criticism; it is easy to become defensive as a way of shutting it off. However, what those who feel alienated, rejected, abused, or oppressed have to say is vital input for working to a solution. In addition, we believe that those passionate enough to express their views typically move beyond the critical stage when they sense they are being heard. Their behavior changes; they become more thoughtful in their remarks; they are motivated to work at the solution, if that opportunity is offered. On the other hand, if people do not believe they are heard, listened to, and understood, they will probably never become more than tangentially involved in the church and its mission. A recent program in which we were involved was especially instructive in this respect. People alienated from the church were invited to a listening session. Their concerns were posted, discussed, and acknowledged by people active in the congregation who noted that they too had had similar experiences. The group met several times, and with each discussion, rough edges were smoothed. The alienated saw that all the church could not be so characterized, and leaders heard the pain of separation and areas which they must address.

Conclusion

Effective Christian leaders for today and tomorrow are collaborative leaders. Following the Jesus model, the collaborative leader focuses first on the development of community and team. The wisdom people convincingly do this. Beyond this stage, leaders must develop open and ongoing vehicles for mutual dialogue and shared decision-making. From the lay point of view as revealed by the wisdom people, there are some critical behaviors which should characterize the church leader's interface with the laity. These include, using the expertise of the laity, conveying a sense of their being valued, not perceiving offers of assistance and participation as intrusion, and empowering all to the maximum extent possible.

The next step in developing collaborative leadership is to work assiduously at fostering and supporting the gifts of the laity. This will be the focus of chapter eight.

Reflection Questions

1. Am I convinced of the need for a collaborative approach to leadership?

2. In what ways do I foster the development of community and team?

3. How do I have to change to be more collaborative?

4. Is collaboration more a professed value than lived reality for me?

5. Do I create opportunities for ongoing mutual dialogue and shared decision-making?

8

Fostering the Gifts of the Laity: The Priority of Leadership

> I think one of the greatest tragedies in the church, one of the greatest sins of the church today, is its underutilization of talent especially the talent of the laity.
>
> Joe

Joe's plaintive cry echoes that of a number of the wisdom people. They believe leaders can miss rich opportunities to carry out the church's God-given mission more effectively when they assume an almost cavalier attitude toward the laity. Far too often, laity are seen as passive recipients of ministry rather than as major resources available to the church for ministry and leadership. In the view of the wisdom people, a leader's effectiveness can be measured in terms of how consistently and creatively the gifts of the laity are identified, developed, and used.

The Episcopal church published a bulletin called *The Ninety-Nine Percenter*, the title capturing the reality of the church: ninety-nine percent of Christians are lay, not ordained. This points to the imperative for Christian leaders to involve and animate the entire Christian community as their major priority. The further implication is that most laity are called to use their gifts primarily where they are—in ministry to the world rather than within the organized ministries of the church.

Because most of the wisdom people fill leadership roles in their professional lives, they know their effectiveness is dependent on their ability to identify and engage the skills and talents of those they lead. Indeed, one of the activities industry is absorbed with today is devising systems to determine the competencies (a popular term for abilities or skills) of people on their staffs. This enables managers to assess developmental need and allows them to move people to positions where they will make maximum contributions. It helps employees understand what skills they might learn to enhance their opportunities for growth and advancement.

Knowing that their greatest resources are the talents of their employees, the wisdom people deplore the underutilization of laity's gifts by the church. Certainly church documents enunciate the fundamental principle that all the baptized are called to use their gifts to extend the kingdom. The problem is that too often individual leaders do not act on that principle in their behaviors, attitudes, planning, and decisions.

Recommendations Regarding Gifts

The wisdom people's recommendations to church leaders regarding identification and use of gifts are far-ranging:

- Recognize, acknowledge, and value the gifts of the laity.
- Support the use of their gifts in ministries outside the church.
- Help to develop gifts and involve laity much more intentionally and vitally in the mission of the church, with special emphasis on their gifts for leadership and teamwork.
- Empower the laity to utilize their gifts, creating an environment where people feel called to contribute to the fullest extent possible.

Gifts and Responsibility

We found that the wisdom people were quite comfortable discussing their gifts. This was not surprising considering their reflective approach to life. For many, what the interviews did was to help them recognize how strongly they use their gifts day-to-day; it reinforced their awareness of their occupation as their personal ministry. These are not people who avoid responsibility; rather, it grows from awareness of their giftedness and from their understanding of their Christian call. While their strength lies in their taking action based on their personal commitment, they do express frustration that some church leaders are negligent in not giving their people more help in identifying, developing, and using their gifts effectively.

Joe, quoted at the beginning of this chapter, summarizes what many of his peers maintain, "I know there are incredible amounts of talent out there that we're not touching."

Frat speaks of the "basket" of gifts and talents he, like every other Christian, possesses.

> Each of us has a basket with some gifts and talents in it that have been given to us, that we haven't earned and that are a piece of God himself. And each of us is absolutely, positively unique. There is never another you, never will be, never was. So our gifts and talents, the blessings we have been given, are in our basket and the Lord is constantly saying to you, me, and everyone, "Will you share your gifts and talents with my friends?"
>
> I know what God has given to me. I didn't earn it and didn't deserve it, but I have to give it away.

The relationship between recognizing personal gifts as free endowments from God and the responsibility to use them in service to others is a theme that runs through many of the conversations with the wisdom people. They exude a sense of life and generativity as they speak of this combination of gifts and responsibility.

Anthony echoes Frat's words, speaking of his sense of gratitude and responsibility:

> I wanted to give a lot of myself because I thought I had been much blessed. We've all been given certain kinds of gifts...and we have to find ways to use those advantages to help others.

Peter uses his gifts in a responsible way by working with a corporation he helped to establish which makes affordable housing available to low-income people. He remarks:

> Our lives are really to share, and I like to think that I approach life and particularly business by giving something back for everything I've gotten. I'm more focused on serving others through real estate. I feel blessed. I want to share that, to give back something to make the world better than when I found it. It sounds kind of corny, but I feel that I've picked up certain gifts or skills in the real estate business that I can share.

A few years ago, Colman and his wife wanted to use their free time in a way that would combine their personal gifts with their dedication to world peace. They decided to teach courses on peace-making at both the high school and college levels. When we accompanied Colman one evening to one of his courses, he explained one of the central messages he tries to convey to the students:

> Everybody has a call. One of the things I try to tell these people is: "You all have gifts, and college ought to be a time to figure out exactly what those gifts are. And then, go use them in some way."

Jack expands the notion of gift, suggesting how overcoming the negative can enrich the positive. "Being a recovering alcoholic is a wonderful gift." It gives him a completely different understanding not only of himself, but of the people he encounters everyday in the marketplace. He reflects that his alcoholism has opened him to be a more Christ-like, compassionate, ministering person. The healing wound is the gift.

Ambivalence Regarding Ministry in the Marketplace

While many clearly see their gifts and their obligation to use them in workplace ministry, there persists a sense of higher and lower order ministries. There is an ambivalence which runs through the interviews about the importance and value of certain activities as compared with others. This became clearest when, after expressing personal convictions about their own ministry, some made deprecatory remarks when comparing that ministry with the work others do in responding directly to the needs of the poor and suffering. The wisdom people struggle with a number of concerns ranging from personal power to the material comforts they enjoy.

Arthur embodies this ambivalence. In addition to teaching, he uses his skills and influence to effect social change in under-developed countries. But the intellectual, somewhat indirect approach he uses nags at his sense of wanting to see positive results more quickly. Acknowledging his university role as his ministry, he still grapples with its relative importance:

> I'd really feel a lot easier if I could go down to the Catholic Worker House. I think that's what Christianity is. It's basically, eventually a one-to-one approach. In a sense I see what I am doing as a cop-out.

Anthony is a dedicated doctor who recognizes the personal sacrifices he makes for his patients, sacrifices involving both financial gain and time away from his family. He also alludes to the guilt he experiences:

> Maybe it is a cop-out. It's easier for me to do what I am doing. I sit comfortably here doing what I know how to do. I am impressed with the people who take risks, adventure into new areas, and I have never done that. In some ways I've chosen the easy way.

It is interesting that both Arthur and Anthony both use "cop-out," when assessing themselves and their choice of ministry. Their ambivalence is fed by a persistent sense of guilt that theirs is an easier path than that of others.

Mark shares his quandary. He sometimes wonders whether what he is doing to provide fair employment for thousands of people and to enhance the economic stability of their lives is as important as what someone like Mother Teresa is doing. His response: "I can't answer that."

Chris, influencing the values and lives of both his employees and clients, admits the same ambivalence. We asked whether he thinks what he is doing is as important as working with the mentally handicapped or with the dying, two activities he had alluded to. He is uncertain and says that, with his own ministry being so rewarding and fulfilling, he experiences some guilt.

> It's not as heroic. I have a roof over my head. I get three squares. I lead a privileged life. I'm well remunerated for what I do. It's allowed me to have a nice life, get my kids educated, live a fairly comfortable existence.

One of the things that is helpful to Chris, as he tries to resolve this ambivalence, is the challenge presented to him by a mentor he had early in his career. Working in the publishing field during the 1960s, Chris was offered a job which would have involved him in the civil rights movement in the South. While he considered accepting the offer, the man he describes as his mentor and friend called him and asked, "What the hell are you doing?" His question challenged Chris to assess the good he was accomplishing at the time. The mentor pointed out that the witness of fairness, justice, and other gospel values which Chris was giving was exactly what people in the workplace needed to see. The result of the challenge was Chris's coming to a greater appreciation of his ministry:

> It's a ministry. It's a mission. If you try to do it with some equity, some fairness, then I think you are implementing the gospel. There's always that sense, if you're not out like Mother Teresa or in the Peace Corps, or out on the fringe giving witness, you're not really doing important ministry. The belief is that that is where the real heroic witness is. I don't disagree with that, but I just think there are a lot of people quietly going about their business in the trenches. It's a better world because they do their work and try to apply those values and keep people employed.
>
> I don't know if there could be any more satisfaction than knowing you're helping keep sixty people employed and getting their kids through college and all that.

The lesson Chris learned resulted in a keener understanding of the value of keeping alive a business which provides jobs in a moral and ethical work environment and which enables people to feel positive about themselves and their contributions. It is interesting to speculate what the typical church leader might have suggested to Chris had he turned there for help.

Even with this early learning, Chris admits that there are still times when he feels tempted to leave his present position and take a job working for the mentally handicapped or some similarly socially-directed employment. The attractiveness of a job that provides more immediate feedback persists for Chris, as it does for others we interviewed.

The ambivalence we have been discussing is fed, we believe, by some fundamental attitudes about ministry within the church. Chris, for example, believes he would get more support from the institutional church if he were to leave corporate life and move into social work. He questions whether the church sees what he does as real ministry. While he senses support from the broader church community, that is, from the people of God who are in circumstances similar to his, his conviction is that the institutional church is too absorbed with its own sponsored ministry and organizational concerns to appreciate "what's going on out in the trenches." He remarks wistfully that he would love to hear someone do a decent homily on the theme of "render unto Caesar," believing it could help him and others with the tension experienced between making money and living the gospel. But, he declares sadly, "I've never heard it".

We believe that many of the wisdom people are ambivalent about the value of their workplace ministry because of lack of affirmation from Christian leaders. If Chris, Mark, Anthony, and Arthur were to encounter leaders who revealed an appreciation of the roles they play, their dedication to that ministry would be strengthened.

Further Reflections From the Wisdom People

Certainly, many people have an awareness of their gifts and feel called to use them in the service of the gospel. Where they sometimes have difficulty is knowing just how those gifts might be used. Unlike the wisdom people who have strong leadership skills, are committed to forms of ministry in the workplace, and act quite independently, these people are looking for help and direction as to how they might fulfill their Christian vocation. It is in this area, the wisdom people suggest, that effective leaders play a critical role: helping people understand the depth and breadth of their gifts and showing creative ways in which they can be employed. Leaders can also tie utilization of gifts to achievement of other goals. We know, for example, that there is compelling scriptural foundation for understanding God-given gifts, particularly in the letters of Paul. Identifying and celebrating gifts, therefore, can be integrated with a deeper understanding of scripture while exploring people's gifts in group settings can be used as a powerful way to build community.

When gifts are not identified and acknowledged, typically one of two things happens: the gifts languish from neglect, or people experience low self-esteem, feeling that their gifts are nothing special. If people offer and their gifts are not accepted, hurt and anger are often the result. The leader's role, therefore, is to be especially sensitive to gifts and to ways of engaging them for the building of the kingdom.

Church organizations will be successful in direct proportion to how leaders engage laity to use their gifts.

Fostering and Supporting Ministry in the World

Too often it seems that the gifts of the laity appear to be valued only when they are used in direct service to the local congregation. If people choose to be involved in liturgical life, educational endeavors, or the administration of the congregation, they are not only valued, but affirmed and rewarded. People feel that the same response is not forthcoming when their primary ministry is bringing Christ's presence to the world, that God is calling them to minister in the marketplace where they most faithfully respond to their vocation.

Grace puts it beautifully when she describes the attitude she carries to work each morning, "It's my walk with God. It's where I make my contribution, where my audience for God [is]!" Her theology of work is one built on a personal philosophy of service, reflective of her deep faith and convictions.

> Work is supposed to give honor and glory to God. I believe that the opportunity to work is an opportunity to give a manifestation of the human value of God's handiwork. As we go about doing this, we should not be doing it in our own little slots. We should be going about this by coming together to give glory and honor to God. I think it would be a much more vibrant, healthy environment if people worked with that ever present in their minds.

Grace's remarks recall those of a lady we once met who described the desk in her office as her altar. It was there that she daily dedicated her day to God, that she confessed and reconciled, that she sacrificed, that she celebrated life, and that she delivered messages of God's love to others. Is this the image that most Christian leaders carry about the workplace? How might they contribute to the "vibrant, healthy environment" Grace speaks of? What might Christians accomplish if they were to hear the message of marketplace ministry preached more forcefully in their churches and felt supported in their vocations by the church's leaders?

Chris echoes this sentiment when he declares, "I think of business as a vocation." Yet, he adds:

> Christian teaching seldom seemed to address the moral and ethical issues that I face as a manager, I can

recall only one homily that had anything really
relevant to say concerning the issues a manager faces.

In addition to the need for church leaders to address the moral
and ethical issues which Christians face in the marketplace, the
wisdom people provide some specific ideas, aimed largely at empowering people and helping them accept and live their Christian
responsibilities. Reflecting on their own experience and that of
others, they speak of a sense of isolation they sometimes feel in a
work environment where values differ from theirs. They comment
that they are frequently unaware of other Christians who nurture the
same hopes and dreams and who struggle with similar day-to-day
issues. They urge church leaders to:

- Provide opportunities for people to talk with each
  other and extend mutual support as they struggle
  with their Christian values in the marketplace.
- Speak to the needs of Christian managers and executives in the same prophetic and forceful ways that
  church leaders have more frequently addressed the
  needs of workers.
- Stress the unique opportunities for positive change
  which the laity has available through their roles in the
  world.
- Affirm people in the primacy of their vocation and
  ministry, not comparing these unfavorably with
  church-sponsored ministry.

The kind of church leadership the wisdom people expect was
that demonstrated by the National Catholic Conference of Bishops
issuance of the pastoral on the economy in 1986. This was the one
church document people cited when asked about current influences
on their values. Clearly, there was not universal support for the
pastoral's content; some people felt it was one-sided because it did
not address the role of the employer with the same sensitivity and
compassion with which it addressed worker issues. The positive
value of the letter, however, came from the challenges it raised,
providing grist for personal reflection and group debate about the
relationship between Christian principles and the daily lives of
thousands of people. Sadly, it was not a document often talked about
in homilies. While the bishops showed moral leadership, local
church leaders generally allowed it to pass with little involvement

from their congregations. Still, the letter stands as a beacon of hope for some. As Mark says:

> I was always very much excited by Catholic encyclicals on labor. I would hope that we can get as excited about some of the issues facing management as Christians as we were in the period from the 1890s, right through the end of World War II with respect to labor issues. I think those battles have been pretty much fought, certainly in the United States. That is not true in other parts of the world. To the extent that we can now address some of the very exciting issues for Christians in business as they take on roles of broader responsibility...if we can bring some excitement in terms of the application of Christian teaching to management issues, I think it is going to be great for Christians in business. But it's also going to make the church more exciting and a more responsive institution for those within it.

When we conduct workshops on ministry, most church leaders give intellectual assent to the proposition that ministry in the marketplace is at least as important as ministry within the church. However, as discussion continues, it often becomes apparent that acceptance of this proposition is rather superficial. And moving from an intellectual acceptance to an operational one is a long and difficult journey. Thus, there remains a perceived hierarchy of ministry: what one does in and for the church is more important than what people do for their families, communities, and places of business. The need for transformation from this mode of thinking is compelling. Resistance comes from the well-intentioned, but narrow focus of some church leaders for whom preservation of the institution is preeminent. This too often blocks them from seeing the broader purpose of the church to help people live their individual vocations in accordance with Christian principles.

Gretchen speaks of the positive steps her church takes to convey that each member's obligation is to carry Christ's message to the world. The ceremony she describes obviously speaks as powerfully to those leaving the congregation as to those who remain:

> I also wish they would stress more, and this is my own bias, that our job is to be out there...our job is not to ignore the homeless. It is not to ignore the

immigrant. It is really to live our faith in our own homes. We really have to mirror Christ who chose to live his life in the world, not in isolation. He said, "I must be about my father's business," and I really think that message isn't said often enough to the community. When someone leaves our community, they are generally asked to stand, and the church is asked to respond to them, to send them out. And the last words are: "We send you out to be Christ to the world." And I think that is the central message. I don't think it does any good to be Christian just in my intellectual soul. I think unless we live it, it hasn't any value. It is only an ego trip.

Further Reflections on Support

While the wisdom people call for regular and ongoing support from church leaders, most are not optimistic that the situation will change significantly. They advocate, therefore, that the laity themselves take the initiative to create supportive structures. Chris speculates:

> I don't find a whole lot of support [in the church]. I don't find any place to go. There's no group of business people that the church would get behind and help with the development of some kind of peer ministry. Maybe it's something we should do ourselves and not wait for the institutional church.

We can read this statement in two ways. It can be seen as a form of empowerment on the part of laity: they will create vehicles which support their life needs. But it can also be viewed as a further criticism of the church: it is out of touch and unable to meet the needs of its people.

Dawne, in her practical way, perhaps suggests a viable approach. She has been involved in her diocese with the formation of both ecclesial and marketplace ministers. Speaking from the perspective of what she has seen that is successful, her suggestion is rather simple. If people are going to grow in their faith commitment and be creative and effective in carrying their beliefs to the world, either the laity themselves or church leaders need to convene and encourage them to "tell their stories" to one another. It is her view that in the telling and listening, people will find the support and strength they need for their ministry.

Robert comments that if he and others are to be true to their Christian vocation in the world, they need regular reinforcement of that vocation in the preaching and teaching of the church. He needs to hear that "it is worth doing the right thing and that I am not alone". It is the theme of feeling alone in a complex and fast-paced world that appears to prompt the call for connection with a group of like-minded people. Robert's bias is that teaching and preaching focused more on important gospel values and ministry, rather than on sexuality, would foster personal empowerment and encourage people to strengthen their Christian commitments.

We believe that whether or not people receive support and encouragement from church leaders, they will continue to minister actively in the workplace. The question is how long their energy and enthusiasm will be sustained without affirmation and the power which flows from hearing how gospel values inform all aspects of life. This was the point Bishop Hubbard, in the pastoral letter mentioned earlier, was making when he urged parishes to acknowledge and celebrate ministries of service to the world and society, not just those which foster parish development.

Lay Leadership

An interesting distinction that became apparent in the interviews is the gap between lay ministry and lay leadership. The enormous gifts of the laity have to be channeled not only into service and ministry, but also into leadership. While many church leaders are relatively comfortable with the concept of lay ministry, there is not generally a corresponding acceptance of the concept of lay leadership. When leaders are secure enough to appreciate and tap the unique leadership qualities and gifts of the laity, the church will be richer. Grace puts it very concisely. "The church needs to be better about empowering and sharing the leadership in the church with lay leaders." She speaks from experience as a leader within her own profession as well as one attempting to expand lay leadership within her diocese. In both areas she attempts to bring the same values of fairness, generativity, and integrity. Discussing lay leadership, she comments that there is "too much literature not supported by action," stating that if the church is serious about wanting lay leaders, they "need to empower them and entrust them with responsibility. Many [church] roles..." she says, "could be carried on effectively by lay leaders." After identifying a number where she believes lay leaders would typically be more effective than clergy and members of religious congregations, she concludes, "When we talk about encouraging lay leaders to assume responsibilities, many times obstacles are set in their way by the very people who called them to that role." It is evident that Grace speaks from personal experience.

The negative side of seeing church people fill leadership roles for which they are inadequately prepared is reflected in the comments Jack makes:

> One of the things that used to drive me nuts, and it still does to some extent, is that the church very often tries to get into areas where it has no expertise, and instead of calling on some of the lay people who have expertise, people with large egos sort of bull ahead and decide they're going to decide how to do it. And they make a shambles of the whole situation where it could have been done better.

We believe that people "bulling ahead" into areas where they have limited expertise is directly related to their own limited sense of self-esteem. All too often, leaders within the church—like many other people—attempt to build and maintain their self-esteem through their work accomplishments. There is no room for them to admit their own inadequacies and turn to others for wisdom and expertise. Rather, they move ahead and achieve ineffective results, causing others to have even less confidence in them. Their behavior is personally and pastorally destructive and ultimately discourages others from working with them, thereby depriving the ministry of the diversity of gifts which reside within the community.

Pat talks about the frustration she experiences when church leaders fail to acknowledge and use the gifts of the laity in ministry. She grieves for the good that goes undone because of this failure to recognize and value the "unique contributions" which could be made. "I think that it is a whole source of gifts and talents that just is not tapped into." Others interviewed relate stories of having volunteered to relieve pastors and church leaders of administrative tasks, only to have their offers interpreted as intrusive.

Peter proposes a series of questions which might serve as a reflection tool for pastors or leaders. Responses to these questions could lead to less frustration for both the leaders and the laity.

> Do pastors accept parish boards? Do they really want lay participation or do they perceive that as intrusion? Does the organized church have faith in its members? Do they want the participation? Can they accept participation? Can they accept criticism or is it safer not to get involved? Do they want to hold on to things the way they have always been?

Peter concluded by saying, "Democracy is painful."

Perhaps the interviewee who evidenced the greatest frustration with church in this respect was Frat. He describes his disappointment when he learned what the fullness of his Christian vocation entails from people other than church leaders.

> My frustration is that so many people will live, search, and die without being opened, without having that message given them, without being empowered by the church. I'm furious with the hierarchy of my church. The reason that I am furious is I have learned what it is to be empowered, but they didn't empower me. And I think that is a terrible waste of a beautiful ideal. That is their job: to empower lay people to live this life of grace, this life dedicated to God in every respect however you can live it. That is what they are supposed to be teaching. They are supposed to be inviting us to do that, to be that kind of person, but they don't.

Not everyone places the blame for lack of utilization of the laity's gifts on church leaders. Sharon talks about being amazed when she encounters people competent in the business world who "diminish themselves" when they enter a church. They fail to acknowledge their own gifts and assume a passive stance of subservient inadequacy. They have apparently never stopped to examine their own behaviors and to recognize that they are the church and have responsibility for its direction. Utilization of lay gifts is, therefore, a challenge for both church leaders and the laity. Both sides, in their own way, are probably at fault for what is not yet a reality.

A primary focus for leaders who want to be more effective is to explore what frustrates the laity in their attempts to collaborate with church leaders. Once the frustrations have been identified, leaders can strategize to overcome the obstacles which exist.

Conclusion

Effective leaders value the gifts of the laity, seeing these as primary vehicles for transforming the world. There are already a great number of people aware of their gifts and their responsibility to use those gifts for others. What they hope for are leaders who will support them in finding ways to make their gifts available for the kingdom.

Among the things leaders can do to foster the gifts of the laity are: overcome whatever is causing frustration, foster lay leadership as well as lay ministries, and encourage and support the ministries of the laity in the world.

Reflection Questions

1. In what ways do I concretely affirm the gifts of the laity?

2. How do I discover the frustrations which impede people's using their gifts in ministry?

3. Do I specifically and consciously encourage lay leadership as well as lay ministries?

4. What are the ways in which I can learn more about ministry in the workplace and affirm those whose call to ministry resides not in church, but in the marketplace?

9

Responding to Needs: The Secret of Leadership

Leadership should be born out of the understanding of
the needs of those who would be affected by it.

Marian Anderson

A basic psychological principle is that behavior is directed by needs. If we want to understand our own behavior or that of others, we should concentrate on needs because they lead us to action—or inaction. While many theorists have defined what they believe are basic human needs, we find Abraham Maslow's most helpful and convincing. Maslow argues that if we are to survive in a healthy way, we need to feel safe and secure, to belong and be loved, and to maintain our self-esteem.

Effective leaders are those who "think needs." They realize they have the greatest impact when they respond to what people really yearn for. A foundation for all that they do, as we discussed earlier, is to listen. Through a patient and time-consuming listening process, they discover needs which are the true motivators of both individuals and the community. It was against the backdrop of the importance of needs that we reflected on all that we had heard in our interviews with the wisdom people. What is it that drives their behavior? Given their strong commitment to be generative and to act with integrity, we concluded that their primary need is to maintain their self-esteem. They live and act in truth, and they constantly respond to the needs of others as a way of answering God's call. Doing this, they feel good about themselves; they are honest to both God and themselves. Were they to act contrary to their values, their self-esteem would be seriously damaged.

In the course of the interviews we determined what needs were articulated or implied by the wisdom people. Two emerged as dominant: the hunger for community and the hunger to have the Good News communicated, preached, and lived in a way that touches their lives and motivates them to be more faithful Christians. These are clear and unambiguous messages to leaders.

The Need for Community

The primary hunger is for community. While working with eighteen parishes in Ireland, we requested that each one conduct a needs assessment. When we gathered to listen to the findings, the representatives of one parish admitted that they seriously considered not conducting the survey. Because of the high unemployment rate, running at almost twenty-five percent of the adult population, they were convinced that any survey would be superfluous. The number one need would obviously be employment. In spite of their conviction that they would gather no additional significant data, they conducted the needs assessment. To their amazement they discovered that the primary need identified by more than fifty percent of the people was not related to employment. It was the feeling of loneliness! The need was for community.

The need identified is not distinctive to Ireland. It is universal, perhaps so pervasive that it is not given much attention in our society. "That's just the way things are." We had an interesting experience here in the United States. A woman in the southwest who was attending a workshop we were conducting waved the stub from her pay check and called our attention to a notation that read, "Loneliness pay; ten percent differential." Her job is to sit in front of a computer screen for forty hours a week, having no contact with other people during those long hours. Like many jobs, this one is solitary with the focus on the person-machine interface, not on a person-to-person relationship. In this woman's case, the company recognized the issue by providing supplemental pay. What they could not provide was community.

Because faith is built in a supportive community, the wisdom people speak of the crying need to bring people together if they are to grow to the fullness of their Christian vocation and ultimately act upon their Christian values in the places they live and work. How Christian leaders listen to this hunger for community and respond is a major challenge.

Dawne reflects on the acute need for community which exists among members of her parish. "We need each other." Her viewpoint is that we are pilgrim people searching for direction, and we will only discover answers when the church creates communities where people can come together "to share our questions." Recall her remarks quoted earlier when talking about vision. Dawne dreams of "safe havens" created by churches to allow and encourage people to do exactly that, to share their questions. It is her conviction that "the church will flourish" where such safe havens exist. "Unless we hear from each other, we will never hear the truth." The leaders of the parish are the designers of the safe havens, creating circles of mutual respect and trust, so that all—leaders and members—can share their questions and feel they have been heard.

These safe havens, however, are not meant to protect and shield Christians from encountering and engaging with the larger world outside. Christian community is, by its very nature, expansive. It must insert itself into the larger community. Church organizations whose focus is primarily or exclusively internal are no longer Christian communities but are an enigma and contradiction.

Raymond argues for church communities which are sensitive and responsive to the crying needs of the people who live in the neighborhoods surrounding the church. He believes in a Christian community which is aggressive, mission-oriented, and willing to take risks.

> Go out of your perimeters and touch the people that need to be touched. Don't get into your own clique and stay within your clique. Church people hang out with church people, cops hang out with cops, reporters hang out with reporters. Go out of that perimeter and bring those people into the house of the Lord and heal those people.

The passion of his statement is striking. He challenges the inward focus, challenges people's deeply-ingrained habit of talking only to those whom they know personally or with whom they agree. Consider the Jesus model as described in chapter two. Did he speak only to the religious? To the rabbis? To those in specific trades and occupations? To only those who thought as he did? His peripatetic wanderings brought him into relationship with all kinds of people and widely-varied viewpoints. He was able to bridge differences by getting to the elemental hungers he heard people express.

Nancy suggests that most churches, through their weekly services and liturgies, have unique opportunities to provide people with what they need and are seeking. In her remarks, she links the need for community which we have been discussing with the importance of preaching so that the word of God both excites and challenges the gathered community:

> I think the Church's mission should be to use the Sunday liturgy, making that as good a community experience as possible. I continue to believe that this kind of liturgy is the key to Christian life. For many people it's going to be their once a week contact, formal contact, with a group of Christians, so I think it's really essential that it be a relevant experience to people. A great deal of preparation should be given to the proclaiming of the word and homilies. It's too bad sometimes that the quality of Sunday liturgies is uneven. I think it's really important, not just to entertain people, but to make it a real celebration that is uplifting and at the same time challenging for people.

People are hungering for community, a faith community which will satisfy not only their needs for affiliation but their needs to grow in the knowledge of the Lord. Leaders, therefore, will be most effective when they integrate the two, using community to deepen people's understanding of the word and using the word to build community.

The Need to Be Fed by the Word of God

The second major hunger which the wisdom people identified is the need to be fed with the word of God. Preaching is probably the most significant way in which ordained ministers communicate with their communities. Segments of a parish might gather for a meeting or social event where leaders can gain insight into the lives and needs of its members. It is the Sunday service, however, that draws the whole community. Through the homily, the leader has the opportunity to convey the fact that he or she has truly listened. The themes which are chosen, the stories that are told, the metaphors chosen, and the conclusions reached all convey to the community that the preacher is sensitive to and understanding of the issues they are dealing with. The function of the homily is to take the word and apply it to the lived reality. Thus, on two levels, the homily is a reflective process—reflective on the needs and issues of the community and reflective on the scripture. The marriage of those two is the province of the minister. That is how the minister significantly contributes to both the life of the community and to the lives of individual members.

This is the context out of which the wisdom people speak. Their emphasis on the need for preaching which is both responsive and which points to new directions is touched on again and again. Clearly, they feel a lack in the preaching they are currently hearing. They are calling for change. They hunger to hear the word of God made personal and vital.

What follows may be construed as being solely for those whose ministry includes formal preaching. But we recommend that all who minister collaboratively —both preachers and others in church ministry—would benefit from meeting together to reflect on what is being proposed by the wisdom people. Through a corporate discernment of this sort, greater insight into needs and responses can emerge for all. Additionally, such discussion can help to assure that there is alignment between what is being preached and what is being done in the church through its formal ministries.

Hillman, probably reflecting on his own background as the son of a Southern Baptist minister, speaks about his expectations of preachers: they are people who explain the word and also move people to action.

> Make sure they really are feeding the sheep. The sheep out there are hungry, and they need feeding. It means giving them the word, explaining the word and making sure the word is activated. Make sure you put them in a position to do certain things in addition to teaching them. Direct them in certain areas to effect social change. The church can do that through its membership. The church can first of all educate its members about the different problems out there and how religion can be used, the values can be used to address those problems.

What might be surprising in this context is the emphasis on sheep and shepherds certainly not the typical or comfortable metaphor for most people today. But, interestingly, others, like Jim, use the same image:

> I would like to see pastors concentrate on being
> shepherds. I think they need to concentrate on prayer
> and being shepherds, and on homilies that deal with
> what we are facing out there in the world.

What is behind this emphasis on shepherd which seems to
convey the image of a wise, knowledgeable shepherd herding dumb
and passive sheep? This is not the image suggested by the wisdom
people. An experience in Ireland probably best explains it. While
there, our host was driving us across seemingly endless fields dotted
with grazing sheep. He made an observation that often escapes city
dwellers: shepherds lead from the rear. They are not up front with
the sheep following submissively behind, but instead at the rear
encouraging and cajoling. This model of leadership recalls the cryp-
tic description of leadership proposed by Alexandre Lendru-Rollin,
a French Revolutionary leader, who observed, "There go my people.
I must find out where they are going so I can lead them." Good
shepherds lead by listening and responding. When those we interviewed spoke about a relationship of sheep and shepherd, it was
consistent with this pastoral approach.

Jim also identifies very practical ways of "feeding people" by
helping them deal with the realities of their own lives. One of his
own leadership concerns is to convince people to, "Bloom where you
are planted!" If people could fully embrace that wisdom, they would
value themselves more and be more life-filled and life-sharing Christians. He goes on to say that he believes many Christians have
illusory concepts of what constitutes the fullness of Christianity. His
hope is that people might come to realize they are fulfilling Christ's
mission when they enter their place of work each day.

> It is not easy to be taught that—and it's very easy to
> run and become a missionary. If you engaged in
> explicit missionary work, you feel like you are doing
> work that is gratifying and you are saving the world.
> There is plenty of saving to be done in the
> marketplace. People need to be taught that.

Through his job in the building trades, Jim has a positive impact
on a great many people, using his contacts to involve other professionals in housing for the homeless. He talked about how he is
sometimes tempted to leave construction and work exclusively with
the homeless. He went so far as to explore the idea with a colleague
and friend who suggested that if there were one thousand people

homeless when Jim quit his job to work with them full-time, eventually there would be "one thousand and one homeless." The logic of his friend's reply links directly to Jim's own advice about people blooming where they are. His friend advised him:

> You need to concentrate and use your time and your contacts to help the homeless. And that's a real ministry. Do your work and still try to reach people there.

The temptation returns often because, "It's hard being in the marketplace." Jim wants and needs shepherds who will hear his struggle, reminding him of his primary obligation to be a Christian in the workplace and reinforcing the importance of his calling.

People desire preaching that transmits a message that has relevance to their lives. They are not interested in general pious messages and oversimplified retelling of the gospel stories. This is certainly a theme picked up by Dawne who speaks of her need to hear homilies which are relevant to her experience and the issues with which she grapples as a Christian in the marketplace.

> Many times the homilies are kind of packaged. They are not coming out of a life experience that people can relate to, and I don't think that the people giving the homilies, whoever they may be, need to be in the workplace. I don't think they have to be behind a desk in order for people to relate to what they are saying. I think our experiences are common enough. So all I think they need to do is spend a little bit more energy relating that to their own struggle and then sharing that in relation to whatever the gospel message is for that day. Then all of us will come out with something.

Robert speaks of his hunger for good preaching and his frequent frustration and disappointment with the content of most of the sermons he hears.

> To me, preaching is very important. We need support. The best thing that I can hear or that I can experience is that it is worth doing the right thing and that you are not alone. In other words, the milk toast, wishy-washy, B.S. [of sermons that] try to be acceptable, I think, is the worst thing the church can do. I think it has to be sensitive and caring of all its faithful. Quit being so hung up on the sex thing. I think it's a

complex. I really do think the sex thing just saps so much energy. I mean sex in the broader sense of the word. I think it's got to be incorporated more in the whole body of teaching.

Peter advances the issue even further, asking that affirmation and hope be the underpinnings of preaching, rather than the negative approach so often taken.

I don't think we do a great job of taking the scriptures and applying them to daily life. I know we hear a lot of heady stuff, and I still think we hear a lot of negative stuff. You know the church is still to this day on a negative bent, still focusing on sin, a lot of "don't do this" and all that. It really needs to be more related to the fact that we are the people of God, and focus on the fact that we, each in our own lives—even if you are a person who's at home, handicapped, who can't get out—can still be ministers of Christ in our daily circumstances, whether it's doing phone calls from home or something. You know we can each in our own lives, as limited as they are or as full as they are, be a witness to Christ's message and be a minister or a priest in our daily lives.

He acknowledges that no matter how the message is delivered, many of those in attendance will still not hear it. He realizes that the real impact comes through most clearly and strongly when he is afforded the opportunity to reflect with other committed Christians. He wishes that he might have the opportunity to present that message to a congregation.

Those Ten Commandments—they're all negative. A couple of months ago I said. . . I would love to preach on this. I would turn them around and . . . start with the positive. For example, I have what I need, I don't need to steal. I love my wife, I don't need someone else's. If we could put a positive spin on those ten negatives and turn them into ten positives you could come away from some scripture and say, "I feel pretty good about my life. I thank God for the gifts I've got. I thank God for whatever is opposed to the negative." I think there is too much negative. I know in my life I go to other places where I get the positives.

Kate and Jack, working in the field of communication and media, hunger for better preaching. So important is the homily that they suggest that others beside the clergy be given the opportunity to preach if they have the gift.

> We are a community of people begging to be preached to. There are so few good homilies given in our churches, so few memorable sermons that I think the church is missing a huge, huge responsibility in not teaching priests how to preach. And if they don't know how, let the laity preach, let the sisters preach and let the brothers preach. But to get up on Sunday morning when you have a captive audience for forty-five or fifty minutes and give a dull sermon is sinful.

Others echo this same theme of tapping into the giftedness and wisdom of the nonordained members of the congregation. The discussion about the inadequacy of preaching did not focus on form or delivery but on content. What people seek are messages from ministers who have a rich understanding of life and can reflect on the scripture from the depth of their experiences and insights.

> I would suggest that either they broaden their own life experience or they give permission to tap the wisdom of their community and allow those ethical questions in the real world to be more essential to their message. I need something which is going to give me grist to chew on while I drive to the office. I find the message of Christ very abstract and I have to work hard to translate that into the concreteness of my life.

Eugene, who made the above remarks, describes how the gospel message becomes alive and operable for him when he has an opportunity to dialogue with others struggling with the same issues.

Conclusion

The wisdom people have spoken. They hunger for faith communities that will nurture them and challenge them to be all that they are called to be. They long to be fed by the word of God as it is communicated through those who preach. They identify very specific areas which they need to hear and have reinforced if they are to continue as committed Christians in the marketplace. We believe that they speak, not only for themselves, but for the larger Christian community. The question is simple. Can the leaders hear these pleas and are they willing to respond?

Reflection Questions

1. How do I discover the primary needs of the people I purport to serve?

2. How important is community to the group or organization which I lead or which we are a part of?

3. What can I do to foster the development of supportive faith communities?

4. How can I improve preaching and our understanding of the word of God?

5. How do I integrate preaching of the word with all other initiatives in the faith community? Does community help to deepen understanding of the word? Does preaching help to bring the community closer together and challenge them to compassionate ministry?

10
Influencing Values:
Leaders Supporting Leaders

My values come from observing life and from observing
how God works.

Mirta

Leaders exert influence both directly and indirectly. Our sense is
that most of their energy goes into the former, with what they say
and do helping shape the values and actions of those they lead.
Indirectly, leaders can influence the broader community. This is a
more subtle and elusive form of leadership, but one which is criti-
cally important because it enables the leader's reach to extend to a
far larger circle of people. We suggest it is in the area of influencing
the influencers where more attention is needed. Who are the people
whom leaders should be influencing and supporting so as to impact,
through them, the community at large?

Values are formed through training and teaching, observation of
others, experience, and personal reflection. What is important is how
people use these vehicles throughout their lives to develop and
strengthen their values. For the wisdom people, this is a continuous
process. They constantly refine their values, honing them with the
whetstone of faith. Experiences and situations which might be
devastating for others become sources of wisdom and growth for the
kind of people with whom we spoke.

We believe that gaining insight into values formation will be
helpful to Christian leaders, enabling them to put their energies
where they will have the strongest impact. As leaders in their own
spheres of influence, the wisdom people tell us a great deal about

values and their evolution. Indeed, one of the most fascinating parts of the interviews was when people talked about sources of their values. This chapter, therefore, will describe ways in which people arrived at their values and will talk about the individuals who most profoundly influenced them.

Influences on Values

When we began our research, we assumed that two foundational institutions, the family and the church, would have the greatest influence on the lives of those interviewed. We were correct with the first and, judging from the group with whom we spoke, very much off the mark with the second. Not surprisingly, people believe their values are most significantly shaped by their families. The church, by contrast, was rarely mentioned as a primary, direct source. People did not say that the church was *not* an influence; they simply did not speak of the church with anything like the frequency with which they talked about their families, friends, and others.

One of our surprises is how often the father is named as the primary transmitter of values for both women and men. We cannot say this is true for the general population, but it is interesting that when we share this finding with groups, it typically triggers lively discussion. It is an idea not frequently considered. The result of the debate is that many agree that the role of the father as the major influence rings true to their experience. The mother plays a complementary role, helping to nurture and develop the individual's values.

In addition to parents, other people frequently mentioned are siblings, parent-surrogates, friends, mentors (for male businessmen), teachers, leaders in youth organizations, peers in the workplace (primarily providing exemplary behaviors), and the interviewees' own children. Where church is mentioned, the influence is more often associated with the people of God as a caring, supportive community rather than specific individuals or religious leaders.

Some people did not identify specific people as dominant influences on their values. Instead, they discussed experiences, often traumatic ones, which they lived through and concluded that their values are the result of reflection on those. This is consistent with results of a Gallup Poll taken to determine where people discover truth. Only 3.5% attribute the source to religious leaders. In contrast,

42.6% say that their truth is the result of personal reflection on experience. It is also consistent with what Pope John Paul II stated in his encyclical, *On the Permanent Validity of the Church's Missionary Mandate*:

> People today put more trust in witnesses than in teachers, in experience than in teaching, and [in] life and action than in theories.

Asked whether there were significant incidents which influenced the development of their values, respondents rarely identified any. Values seem to emerge from reflection on cumulative life experiences, rather than from a single, extraordinary event such as a conversion experience like that of St. Paul.

Summary of Findings

- Primary influence on values formation is the family.
- Within the family, the father is most frequently identified as the one who influenced value development.
- Friends, associates at work, and mentors (for businessmen) are strong influences.
- Rarely are religious leaders, programs, or movements the primary influence on values.
- Personal reflection on accumulated experiences has significant influence on one's values.

What this summary fails to convey are the passions and convictions which lie behind the findings. As we talked with people, we touched on powerful undercurrents in their lives which, for some, had not surfaced for years. As a result, this portion of the interview was often a path to further self-discovery. What follows are examples drawn from the interviews which provide clues to areas where leaders might support those who shape values.

Family as Influence

Those who credited both parents as the primary source identified each as having transmitted different values. The complementary nature of these is seen as a real blessing. Frat, a physician whose energy goes into alleviating suffering, made this point as he discussed both his values and those of his siblings whom he characterized as "very compassionate."

> I suspect that all of us in the family tend to be that
> way, and I think that came from my eighty-nine year
> old mother who is a very loving person and who
> really taught me a lot of the values. She taught me the
> value of compassion. My dad taught me discipline
> and honesty and dedication. Between the two, ob-
> viously, I had the best of both worlds.

Hillman, a legislator, has committed his life to win support for
public policy to improve the lives of the less fortunate. He describes
himself as "Christ-centered," trying to bring the values of Christ to
his decisions in the State Assembly. The strong Christian influence
of his family has increasing impact on him today. He describes the
generative approach to life which was communicated by both his
parents.

> I came from a very strong Christian home. We were
> brought up to respect our fellow man, to look out for
> the poor, for the good of the community as opposed
> to looking out for the individual person. I was taught
> that if we looked out for the community, then the
> individual persons would benefit in the process. It
> also centered our life around the church and the
> teachings of Christ and what he stood for as opposed
> to striving for some of the popular mandates.

Although parents were indisputably the family members who
most strongly influenced values development, they were not the
only ones. David, for example, gives a glowing tribute to the aunt
who raised him:

> My mother and father died when I was three years of
> age, and I was raised by a maiden aunt who, at the
> tender age of twenty-eight years, took three kids
> under her wing. I mention that with some emotion,
> as you can tell, because I think that whatever service
> orientation I have felt in my life probably, somewhat
> unconsciously, had its origins in that experience.

Scott gives his children credit for influencing his values. As they
mature he talks with them about his involvements at work. Their
reactions, questions, and comments, he says, "…have a tremendous
influence on me. Some of [my best] ideas come from talking with
them."

While most people spoke of positive family experiences in the development of their values, others described growing up in families where Christian values were either not observed or not believed in. They spoke, however, of being able to draw on the positive where they found it and to learn from the negative.

One woman painfully recounts being sexually abused by her father; yet, when identifying those who significantly influenced her values, she names him in relation to the way she tries to live her Christian commitment in the workplace. Still experiencing pain and anger, she can condemn his behavior in one area, but can concurrently attribute many of her positive values to what he provided.

Gretchen was unequivocal in giving her parents credit for the values which influence her decisions in the marketplace, especially her concern, care, and compassion for her employees. Her family was not Christian; she describes her parents as "avowed agnostics...and political dissidents." She recounts how she and her brother were taunted by their classmates on the way home from school because of their parents' political convictions. The experience taught her to defend herself and her family's values, and she talks of how there were positive results:

> There is a strength that comes out of that; that it is all right to have an opinion different from someone else; that you, as a person, count, and your values count more than society's. The strength of your own convictions allows you to be different, allows you to carry on in your own way.

A man who grew up in a dysfunctional family environment describes the evolution of his own values this way:

> My values come from a reaction to, rather than having been taught. My father was an alcoholic—a profane, violent man. If he had a set of values, I think they were absolute self-indulgence, and I grew up being terribly ashamed of my family, especially of my father. He was an embarrassment time and time and time again. Growing up as a child I felt that very keenly. I determined that I would not be like that. I would never subject children to the things we were subjected to. I would make a contribution in the world, and the world would be better for my having lived in it.

Father as Influence

While the entire family influences the development of values, the father is frequently singled out for doing this in a most significant way. Hillman, for example, talks at length about his father:

> My father is a Baptist Minister, and I spent a lot of my time traveling with him as a child, going from community to community. He did a lot of preaching in the rural areas of the state in some of the small churches. I had a chance to observe the conditions of some of the people first hand—how they were living, some of the things they stood for. My traveling with him gave me the opportunity to hear him preach on a regular basis—love for fellow man and all those things. I think that kind of stuck with me over the years. But in terms of public service, I never thought back then that I would be going in this direction. But I knew that I had some mission and was in the process of preparing myself to do it.

For Hillman, his father clearly had the primary impact on his "mission" of fostering justice and improving life for the poor. It was the opportunity to travel with his father which sensitized Hillman to their plight and ultimately led him to politics as a vehicle to rectify social wrongs. Like many of those interviewed, his emphasis on generativity and integrity had their genesis in the values observed in his father.

Arthur, a university professor, also describes how his travels with his father had a significant impact on his early development. "I'd have to say [that my values came] strongly from my father. He really believed in the dignity of other people." This is reflected in Arthur's life today as he uses his expertise to help underdeveloped countries. This work goes neither unnoticed nor without criticism by some faculty members who feel that a chaired professor should focus his energies more on assisting younger faculty members. Arthur is quick to point out, "I have chosen what I think is important rather than merely meeting their needs." He attributes his concern for the dignity of others directly to his father whose influence he continues to feel. He also attributes his gift for listening to his father, a piano salesman.

> The greatest advantage I ever had was that I travelled with my Dad, two or three Saturdays a month, from

the time I was about six until I was in high school. I had a lot of time to visit with him, and he had a lot of time to listen to me. It was a really incredible relationship...far and away the most important of my younger life.

Perhaps it is his ability to listen that most impresses Arthur's students who have honored him on more than one occasion as an outstanding teacher.

A poignant example of the profound influence of the father is described by Colman, who uses his position as a writer to sensitize others to the plight of the marginalized and oppressed. The formation of his values occurred in his childhood home as he observed the behavior of his father:

> My father was a lawyer on Long Island, and our home was always filled. He took care of immigrants from Eastern Europe, Ireland, Italy, and Greece. The house tended to have people coming through from Ellis Island. I wondered, "How did these people get to be poor and why do they get kicked aside so much, and what can I do about it?" My father was doing something about it, in a small way, taking care of their legal problems, wills, and real estate matters, and just ordinary legal problems.

Seeing his father's concern and compassion for those "kicked aside," Colman had what he referred to as his early "radicalization." He goes on to describe his father as a caring person who did whatever he could to alleviate people's sufferings; he was "a happy man" who did not care about money, giving most of it away and keeping just enough to sustain the family.

The power of the youthful experience on values formation is evident in a story told by Scott who describes the impact of his father's attitudes and beliefs on him. The twenty-year-old Scott was working for his father whose business, still on "shaky ground," was beginning to enjoy some success. Scott and a co-worker, a young black man, were assigned to deliver lighting fixtures to a potential major account. Establishing good customer relations would have significant financial impact on the fledgling business. Returning from the delivery, Scott noticed that the young man was "really, really down." Scott kept "bugging" him about what had happened until finally the employee admitted, "When I took those light fixtures over there, they said, 'We

don't want any niggers delivering here.'" Scott reported the incident
to his father and describes the response:

> He didn't hesitate a second. There wasn't a moment's
> hesitation. He said, "I'm going to go over there right
> now, and they're not going to ever talk that way to
> one of my employees." He went over there and told
> them, "Forget the whole business if that is the way
> you are going to act." Then, the employee they had
> said this to went over there, and they apologized to
> him and said it would never happen again.

When Scott reflects on this incident, he gets in touch with some
important insights which continue to influence him today. He says
he realizes that taking action quickly and decisively is critical; you
have to "do the right thing" even when everything you have worked
for might be in jeopardy. "You have to do that. It's important and
that's the way you have to be." He concludes that the incident not
only speaks about his father but serves as a powerful lesson of what
one must do in similar circumstances. This incident is probably the
ultimate witness for him of what it means to be a person of integrity.
Scott, in turn, is influential today because of his personal integrity,
doing what he believes is right for poor, underpaid restaurant
workers. He journeys with them not only through economic struggles but in efforts to develop their self-confidence, self-esteem, and
self-determination.

Grace provides a most moving example of the father's influence
as she describes how what her father did throughout the community
impacted her and those he reached. He was a teacher who went far
beyond the requirements of his job, even providing financial assistance to those in need. He became a role model, especially to men in
the various barrios, and positively influenced a large circle of people.
To demonstrate her point, she tells of a poignant incident which
occurred when he died :

> The person who broke the news that my dad died was
> a guy who was considered to be an outcast in the
> whole community. He was sort of mentally retarded,
> very unusual to look at. Lots of people turned their
> faces when he was around. When my dad died, he
> came running in and said, "I heard Maestro died.
> That's my dad! He hugged me, he fed me, he took
> care of me. Who will take care of me now?"

For Caroline, it was her father's deep faith-life that was a major influence on her. Today, one of her goals is developing her parochial school as a faith community. Recalling her father, she refers to the depth and witness of his faith, telling of a time when he experienced a failure in business:

> He turned to prayer, never giving up. He witnessed
> to me that the Lord was living in him. His witness
> was so strong. He really was a Christ-like figure for
> me. He really modelled the servant image all the time,
> and that is a key thing for me in my own vocation
> now...I think the church should be a servant church.
> So daddy was a real image of that for me.

A final example comes from our conversation with Raymond, a police officer, who says of his father, "He was committed to his whole family. No matter what we went through, he was always there." He relates an instance when he had disobeyed his father and then suffered an injury. Rather than showing anger or moralizing about how Raymond should have obeyed, his father gave a compassionate response, "just wanting to make it all better." What started as training in obedience ended as a powerful lesson in compassion. Raymond obviously learned about both values from the way in which his father handled the incident.

Families: Implications for Leaders

The role of the parent is obviously dominant in values development—both positive and negative—because of the intimacy of the relationship between them and their children. Most people are thrust into the parental role with little preparation other than what their own family of origin taught them. Religious leaders are in a unique position to support families at critical developmental points, helping parents understand their role in communicating positive values. Ted, asked how the church might help him with the challenges in his life, chose to recall that time when his church and pastor served him best by providing training when he and his wife needed it most. It was in the 1960s when, newly married, they had three little girls to raise:

> That's what I really attribute to the personal growth
> training, classes, participation in groups that we had
> [in this church when my children were young] under
> the first minister here, one of those very unusual

leaders of people, motivators of people, who got us to think about ourselves. That was a difficult time. Those were very difficult years. I think our kids got a lot of values, a lot of benefits, from our having gone through that.

It just happened that both my wife and I felt very strongly about supporting our children when they were growing up. And a lot of that did come through from personal growth time that we spent here in this church in the early years—when the kids were just eight, five, and three—the personal growth issues, related to parenting, positive reinforcement, creativity, offering them opportunities to experience a variety of things so that when they became adults, they knew what they were choosing from.

We relate Ted's story because it was obvious that his pastor and church community had a keen sense of what young parents needed as they undertook raising their children. Ted knew he had a need, but could hardly have articulated it. The personal growth sessions which he attended clearly had a major impact on his life and on his family.

---

1. What are the needs of parents and families today as I carry out my leadership role?
2. How can I help people develop their own values so that they are better equipped to foster the development of Christian values in their children?
3. If the father strongly influences values development, what do I as a leader specifically do to help them be more effective in their role?

Parent-Surrogate Figures as Influencers of Values

In addition to the immediate family members who helped form values, a significant number of the wisdom people identified parent-surrogates as primary influences in their lives.

Paul describes two men who became role models for him, serving as surrogate fathers when he was a teen-ager. Interestingly, it was his pastor and assistant pastor who taught him what it means to be a caring, gentle, compassionate male; however, their institutional roles as church leaders seem not to have been the dominant aspect of their relationship to Paul. In addition to modelling positive male characteristics, they taught him skills for working with groups, skills which provide a foundation for his work today as a management consultant focused on values and work relationships.

Eugene speaks at length about a Boy Scout leader who personified for him many of the qualities of a good father, a person of principle, and someone to be emulated.

> A Boy Scout leader was a primary, positive influence in my life. He was just a superb role model. He was what I thought a father should be a very kind, gentle, caring man, but firm. He would listen; he would help you plan something and not think you were foolish. He had lost a son in a hunting accident when the son was twelve years old. He just became a surrogate father to lots of us that lived in less than perfect home situations.
>
> There was another scout leader...a wonderful man, somebody you could look at and say "Boy, I would like to be like that guy." He was strong but kind and gentle. He taught us the values of caring, sharing and compassion, acceptance of other people's points of view or tolerance for them at least. I didn't know it at the time, but, at the same time he was acting as scout leader and providing all this wonderful, warm influence, he was also dying with cancer. For somebody to be able to get outside themselves that much, with that kind of disease, is just an amazing feat. When I think back on it now, I am more impressed with what that man did than ever.

Gretchen, whose parental influence we discussed earlier, also describes a number of adults who helped shape her values. Specifically, she identifies three women—a scout leader, a member of her church, and a neighbor—from whom she learned quite different things, all of them important to her values today.

> From the scout leader I learned that you could accomplish things bigger than yourself if you worked together, and that there was adherence to a value higher than us as individuals. The woman in the church spent long hours that summer with me teaching me—helping me learn, critiquing things. The

neighbor taught me to sew. I can remember running across the backyard with tears streaming down my face as I put the zipper in upside down for the third or fourth time. She had infinite patience helping me take it out and put it in.

In each of these cases, the adult went out of her way to be there for the child who felt, but could not have articulated, that she was loved, esteemed, and valued. The parent-surrogates' involvements in her life obviously helped Gretchen appreciate herself as a person.

The final example of caring, compassionate adult figures reflects these same qualities. Raymond, whose father was such a powerful influence in his life, was blessed with a second positive influence in the person of his basketball coach. He describes how the coach saw "potential in me that I didn't see in myself." The relationship grew strong as the coach kept affirming the gifts and basic goodness he saw in the teen-ager. He took Raymond to his home for a weekend where the young man experienced a way of life different from what he had in his own neighborhood. He attributes his decision to pull away from the gang he was involved with to the revelation that that visit provided. "He just showed me that there was a way of life other than [the one] I had chosen."

Surrogate Parents: Implications for Leaders

We have spoken a number of times about the difficult challenge for leaders: to influence the influencers of values. Given the examples just cited, leaders might despair of being able to touch the myriad of people who might influence the values of young people. We believe it is here that leaders can use their public role to address the broader society about values formation. Involvement in activities within the community, communicating Christian values and how they translate into day-to-day activity is important to subtly change the fabric of society.

---

1. As a leader, is my commitment to Christian values evident to the broader community? Do I speak publicly and write letters to the local press to help influence community values?

2. Within my church, do I help parents whose children are under the direction of another adult learn ways in which they might dialogue with that adult about the values they want their children to develop?

Mentors as Influence

While the majority of those interviewed speak of people they knew in childhood as the principal influences on their values, a number of businessmen talked about the importance of mentors. Typically, the mentor relationship was formed early in the career, at the time the men were learning how to function in a new, different, and challenging environment. Interestingly, mentors are not identified by women, nor are they named by men in fields other than business.

Chris credits his mentor with much of his personal and professional development. The incident which most significantly captures the impact of the mentor involved the time when the business was in trouble and cost reductions were needed. It appeared necessary to eliminate a department to resolve the financial crisis. He determined that he would keep the group intact, reasoning that it would be virtually impossible for them to find other employment if he were to lay people off. The mentor thus decided to fly in the face of the traditional remedy. He would seek alternate ways to achieve his cost objectives.

What was the impact on Chris? He saw the mentor's values in action. He recognized qualities which he admired and wanted to emulate; he saw decisiveness in avoiding the usual response to such a problem; he saw courage in the mentor's taking a path that did not assure success; and he saw compassion as the motivation for retaining employees. The result was that Chris discovered someone whom he knew he could turn to when he faced similarly difficult decisions. His summary statement tells of the ongoing relationship:

> I went to work for a guy who was a real mentor to me. He had a great influence on my life and still does. When I've got problems, I contact him. He not only has business savvy, but he lives the gospel in the ways he treats his people. He has a guileless approach to business. He just wants to do what he senses is right for people. It's very hard to let people go if you have a very strong commitment to the gospel. Not that I haven't let people go. I have. It's a very painful experience.

Joe similarly credits someone he first encountered during his early years in business. His mentor was not always successful nor did he always make right decisions, but the values were always solid. Not only did Joe's mentor influence him in the past but continues to do so beyond death.

> I try as much as possible to bring his set of beliefs, his
> religious beliefs to the business. Sure he failed a lot,
> but he succeeded a lot, too. He proved to me that you
> could bring these values to a business situation and
> be successful. It was a great gift for me and I think
> that it was a tremendous help as I now run my own
> business. He died ten years ago, but I just feel he is
> still with me in terms of some of the decisions I make.

Talking about this mentor at length, Joe expresses appreciation
for the man he describes as "the most important, single influence
in my life." The learning he achieved links interpersonal and ethical
behaviors with business success. He goes on to develop this idea:

> I think it means treating people with respect, treating
> people with human dignity, trying to do the right
> ethical thing in terms of the do's and don't's and then
> being as successful as hell.

The gratitude that the men feel toward their mentors is touching.
It extends beyond appreciation of their talents to gratitude for the
support and direction which they gave. Those mentored recognize
that in no small way their very identity as ethical business people
came from the mentor relationship.

Mentors: Implications for Leaders

It appears that the impact of the mentor is strong because the
revelation of values comes through the practical, day-to-day
decision-making that developing managers are learning. They are
particularly sensitive early in their careers to indications of "how
things really work." The church leader's understanding of the
dynamics between managers and their peers or subordinates will
help them determine ways in which they can influence values in the
workplace. This might, for example, be achieved through a forum in
which people come to understand the important role they play in
developing an environment where Christian values dominate.

---

1. Do I know people who strongly influence the values of those they work with? What do these influencers need from church leaders?

2. While it appears that men are supported by mentors in the development of their values, where are there similar aids for women? What can I do within the church to help women with values issues in the workplace?

The Church as an Influence on Values

While we noted that the church was rarely designated as a primary influence on values, its positive role always seemed present. It appears that its function as a moral and ethical leader is obvious, and it did not warrant discussion. Implicitly for many, the church "covers the waterfront" so far as values are concerned. Because we asked people about specific values and where they developed, it was perhaps more difficult for them to identify sources within the church. Typically, there were passing references to church or church-related schools as places where values were instilled, but few of these conversations focused on individuals. However, two stories bear repeating. The first deals with church leaders who acted in socially responsible ways. The second is the dramatic story of how a minister's intervention gave new direction to a young man's life.

Robert expressed great pride in the role the churches took in supporting the civil rights movement in the South. He credits them and specific ministers with having a positive influence on the development of his own values.

> In growing up in the South and living through the civil rights movement, I was real proud of the church at that time. It was difficult, that eight to ten years in there. It was really extraordinarily difficult, and I am very, very proud of what the Catholic Church of the South did at that time.

Richard relates the story of the transformation which took place in his life because of the intervention of a minister. A poor, young African-American, living on welfare in the inner city, Richard became involved with gang life. One night, he and some of his friends were in the process of stealing a car when their plan was interrupted by a Salvation Army minister. The friends scattered and Richard alone faced the minister. His bravado faded; he was scared, knowing that he could be charged as a delinquent. Wisely, the minister counseled, "You need me, but I also need you. Why don't you come inside and talk?" That visit resulted in Richard and his friends helping the minister start a youth club. He came to realize that this was the beginning of a new life for him. In time he developed as a leader, finding within the church what he was looking for. Not only did the church help Richard to escape the streets, but also taught him "to read and write, to know how to relate to others," and provided him with his first opportunity to serve others. His present work as a management consultant allows him to continue that ministry of service, challenging prejudice and bias in the workplace, and helping people develop skills to be more effective in work and in life.

Church and Values: Implications for Leaders

So much is said and done within the church that relates to values; yet, if our sample is indicative of the larger population, the church's role in values development is not strongly imprinted in people's minds. Does this suggest different approaches are needed? For example, should more explicit value-based education at both the child and adult level be considered? Or, does it suggest that there is insufficient reality-testing of the values promulgated within the church? The words people hear in church are fine, but the experience which validates them occurs elsewhere. Does this possibly link to the earlier comment that the church is seen as out of touch with what is really going on in people's lives?

---

*1. Am I clear about the values I support and am I explicit
about the ways their values operate in daily life?*
*2. Do I feel equipped to work with people on values   clarification?
What might I learn through such a process?*
*3. What is going on within my church that can be used
as practical material for values development?*

Reflection on Personal Experiences

As we introduced the wisdom people, we commented on their openness to discuss times of personal and family crisis and on their ability to be self-reflective. Life's negative experiences do not make them victims. Reflecting on and internalizing crises and painful experiences, they achieve a level of insight and understanding that clarifies and refines the values guiding their lives. As Mirta states in the quote which opens this chapter, this means adopting a stance for observing life through the eyes of faith. She says simply that her values did not emerge from a conscious decision or a sudden revelation. Rather, "I came to an understanding of my values as a result of listening to myself."

Gretchen shares the very personal process through which she reassessed her values, triggered when she was diagnosed as having a malignant tumor. Clearly, her whole attitude to life was impacted, resulting in her undertaking an examination of all its aspects: "...what I do, what I believe in, what I see as valuable in life in general and, in particular, in my own life". She captures what we heard from so many people: the experience of reflecting on personal or family tragedy forces them to reassess their lives and their values, crystallizing and achieving clarity about what is really important to them.

For many, the reflection grows out of workplace experiences which enable them to develop values which guide their treatment of others. Eugene describes how he had been employed in large corporations for almost twenty years before he started his own business.

> In those large corporations, people were not treated with dignity, not treated with respect. They were exploited and used and forced to work under conditions that were less than ideal. They were expected to work long hours, expected to work on weekends without compensation of any kind. I thought that was unfair. They were merely prisoners caught in the system. When I started this company, I thought there must be a way to run a company where you don't do that to people. And so far it has worked.

Others reflect similar reactions to work environments where human values were not given priority. Joe, who now heads a multimillion dollar operation, developed values in reaction to his earlier negative experiences:

> What I experienced in the workplace was causing me physical discomfort, sickness. I was getting upset over some of this stuff that was going on: abusive people, lying and cheating and covering up. It was real bad stuff. I've said the environment I was working in was a cesspool.

As a result, when he became a CEO he did everything possible to build a work environment responsive to the needs of people and conducive to their personal and professional growth. Joe worked with the management team to develop a mission statement for the company which emphasizes its strong commitment to ethics, morality, and integrity.

Others recall childhood experiences as sources for developing their own life philosophy and values. Richard chronicles his personal journey. Growing up as a welfare recipient, he was the victim of ridicule because his family could not afford nice clothes for him. In school he was also degraded. Because he was black, he was told that he was not smart enough to get through high school. In high school, he was told that he would never make it to college. His reaction to this cumulative negativism was a positive determination: "I would never do that to anyone else." Perhaps these experiences were the genesis of his present work in the marketplace as a consultant to help build environments where human dignity is a preeminent value.

Hillman recounts a similar story. Interestingly, he focuses not on what happened to him personally but speaks of seeing maltreatment and injustice suffered by others. He describes people living in abject housing conditions, threatened with eviction, and having little hope because of unemployment. It was then he decided "to better myself so I could be in a position to be of some service to [others] in some kind of way." He declares that these are the driving forces which energize him to make housing one of his major concerns in the state assembly.

The gift of being self-reflective is a dominant characteristic in the lives of the wisdom people, allowing them to grow and develop on a continuous basis. They glean a richness from life experiences which others might overlook or simply endure.

Personal Reflection: Implications for Leaders

Clearly, some people are gifted when it comes to using their personal experience as the basis for intense values examination and development. But everyone can develop skills to reflect on their lives and what it is that drives them. A channel for such development may be offering prayer opportunities in which people can learn ways to examine how God is working in all aspects of their lives.

---

1. Do I personally reflect on life experience as a way of developing my values? In what ways have my values changed as a result?
2. Do I help people to see how their daily experience can be the basis for values development?

Conclusion

Influences on the development of values can come from any number of sources, but our interviews with the wisdom people reveal dominant forces which helped shape their values. As we have seen from the examples cited, these are family members (especially fathers), parent-surrogates, mentors, and reflection on personal experience. The church appears to be a less dominant force than might have been assumed. The challenge facing leaders is discovering ways to influence the influencers and provide vehicles for people to view each life experience as a potential source of growth.

Reflection Questions

In addition to the reflection questions included throughout this chapter, the following general questions may be of help:

1. Who has been the major influence on my values? Have I ever told that person what an influence they had on my life?

2. Are the values of the group which I head evident to both its members and to those who observe its ministry? Is there consistency between what we say and what we do? How do I know that my answer to this question is valid?

III
THE PERSON OF THE LEADER

THE QUALITIES OF **JESUS**	THE QUALITIES OF **A CHRISTIAN LEADER**
A man of integrity	*A person of integrity*
who was authentic and generative	*who is generative and compassionate*
as well as compassionate, forgiving and straightforward.	*and who communicates joy and hope.*

11
Integrity:
The Courage of Leadership

You have to do the *right thing*.

Pat

In the previous ten chapters we focused on what leaders *do* for others. This chapter and those that follow call leaders to self-examination and self-appraisal. What are the personal values and characteristics which are the underpinnings of their leadership? What are the things which they must attend to within themselves? This introspective aspect of leadership is what Edwin Friedman refers to as the "self-definition." Effective leadership is more than just engaging in action-oriented activities. It is a way of positively influencing others through one's own being. This dimension of leadership, therefore, calls for personal insight, conversion, and development.

We believe that the characteristic of effective Christian leadership which precedes all others is that leaders be people of integrity, passionately committed to doing the right thing regardless of the consequences. Effective leaders inspire others by the truthfulness with which they reveal their values through what they say and what they do, and by making clear why they do it. To be sure, these are not easy tasks, especially for Christian leaders whose values are often at variance with those of the world. Yet, they could live no other way. In the final analysis, congruence between what they say and what they do, both in their public and private lives, reveals whether they are people of integrity.

Integrity has been identified as the true crucible of leadership. Through the centuries, it has been leaders' lack of personal integrity which has turned people against them, even when their public actions have had beneficial impact. Mahatma Gandhi declared:

> A leader is useless when he acts against the prompt-ings of his own conscience. To stick to one's guns come what might—this is the essence of the gift of leadership.

The poet, William Butler Yeats, wrote to his son that truth is, in fact, a higher standard for action than are people:

> People think of leaders as devoted to service, and by service they mean that [they] serve their followers. The real leader serves truth, not people.

Ordway Tead in *The Art of Leadership* identifies integrity as an unequivocal characteristic of effective leadership.

> Nothing so betrays the leader as reluctance to stand behind, defend, and pay the price of the course of action he has chosen to follow. He must be willing squarely to shoulder the responsibility; and it is at this point that many people reveal deficiencies which debar them from real strength as leaders.

One of our initial goals was to identify the values which influence the wisdom people's behavior and decisions. We wanted to learn whether there are any values which universally characterize these people regardless of career, geography, gender, or church affiliation. The first ten whom we interviewed established a pattern, with all using almost the same phrase to describe their principal motivation: "You have to do the right thing." They are committed to be people of integrity, faithful to what they believe even when doing so might have serious, negative repercussions. For them, integrity is intimate-ly bound with their very essence.

It is not surprising that one of the wisdom people's principal expectations of Christian leaders is that they, too, be people of integrity. And they expect leaders to reveal that integrity by:

- showing congruence between professed values and lived reality;
- being pro-active and willing to take risks when in-tegrity demands it;
- calling others to high standards of integrity.

Speaking broadly about the church and, implicitly, its leaders, Nancy demonstrates the common gap between theory and practice:

> One thing the church definitely needs to do is to be a little more consistent in terms of practicing the values that it preaches, particularly in terms of just wages for its own ministers, workers, and employees. I think it seems very hypocritical when the bishops will come out with a pastoral on economics and challenge companies out there to a certain standard but then don't practice what the church preaches when it comes to benefits and wages for its own people.

Simply put, this kind of inconsistency results in leaders not being credible. In our interactions with others we may disagree with what they say, but any inconsistency between what they say and do is more troublesome. When this occurs, we lose confidence and lack trust in them. We become guarded and wary of what might happen next. This being true, consider the implications for leaders. Because they are in positions of authority, they are held to a higher standard. Should there be a gap between values stated and actions taken, people are reluctant to follow. Inconsistency erodes credibility. No matter how valid the message, it fails to attract committed followers. When leaders are not people of integrity, they work against the very good they say they want to accomplish. As Eugene noted:

> I think one of the worst things that can happen to church leaders is to profess to believe a certain set of values, but then when you deal with them, you become convinced they really don't believe in those values, because they couldn't be acting the way they are acting if they believed them. I think young people especially are very, very sensitive to that and this tends to alienate many young people from the church.

Typically, the gap we speak of is not apparent to the leader. Self-justification, other pressing demands, and thoughtlessness are likely causes of blindness to their own inconsistency. The results of a research project which dealt with the issue of congruence is illustrative. The subjects, seminarians preparing for ordained ministry, were told by researchers that they were to give a sermon which would be individually videotaped so they could review and evaluate their preaching skills. The assigned text was the parable of the Good

Samaritan. The seminarians waited in a room until a researcher took them, one by one, through a long alleyway to a recording studio in another building. As each passed through the alley, he encountered a man, apparently drunk, lying on the ground, claiming he was in pain, and begging for help. If the seminarian stopped to help, the researcher insisted that they were running late and had to get to the studio immediately. Each of the seminarians went on to the taping, leaving the man for the Samaritan who might chance to come that way!

Leadership Behavior and the Organization

When people lose confidence in their leader, the loss is suffered by the organization; the leader's behavior taints the whole. Richard makes this point in a story about his own experience. As we described earlier, not quite into his teens, he had a transforming experience which took him off the streets and opened church membership to him. The church served as a surrogate family, giving him opportunities to learn and instilling in him strong Christian values. When he was in his early twenties he saw his minister behave in a way that undercut the values being preached. The disillusionment the young man experienced was profound. While he could tolerate mistakes, he could not live with hypocrisy. He left the church, and it was years before he entered another.

> If you tell me something and I believe you, and then I see you do the opposite, I lose faith in you. If you are a minister of the church and you do that, then I lose faith in the church as well. Like I said, I would be a minister today if I hadn't seen a minister do something different from what he was preaching.

In addition to filling a functional role, leaders fill a symbolic one: they become identified with the institution in a unique way. Thus, when the leader acts inappropriately, the negative impact reaches far beyond the individual.

Pro-Active Integrity

Some wisdom people made clear that their concept of integrity means more than merely being consistent with what one professes. For them, people of integrity are pro-active, "doing the right thing" by seeking out the right thing to do, not waiting passively for a situation to present itself. Grace attempts to assume this pro-active stance in her work and is direct in her challenge to church leaders:

> If we are going to guide our people, not only do we participate by speaking out about what is wrong, but we also participate and take risks in those areas where and when it is not a popular position to take.

Another expectation of Christian leaders is that they not only inspire their people to practice integrity individually, they also challenge the entire community to develop its corporate sense of integrity: "What do *we* stand for?" Angel discusses how he found himself increasingly alienated from the institutional church, though not from his God or faith. He attributes this to the lack of integrity he sees not only among church leaders, but also among the broader membership:

> I believe in God and I believe in religion. So it is the organization of religion in which I am very disappointed. I just feel that people and the church itself have gotten very far away from the mandates of God. I don't think that religion is something that you practice on Sunday and that everything else that you do is divorced from religion. I think that religion should be very pervasive in the work that you do, as well as your play.
>
> I think that religion is part of everything in your life and that it should effect everything you do—what you do in the workplace and even in your political life. I can't divorce my religion from my political life. This is where I think the church has had its biggest failure, in separating religion and religious activity. This is why I say that so many of my fellow Christians are hypocritical—they express one thing in religion and another in social, political, and economic behaviors. It leaves a rather bitter taste in one's mouth to see the church preaching one thing but really doing something else.

Paul Wilkes, an author sensitive to the demands on people in ministry, describes what he is looking for in ministers:

> We want them to be people who in some tiny way reflect the mercy and goodness of the God we want

to know, not only his judgment. We want them to be people who see the goodness in us that we have yet to unleash, the potential within us to transcend our differences. In the end, I think, we are looking for those who will help us find that voice deep within us which is not our own, but calls us to do what is right.

For the wisdom people, the highest leadership accolades go to those who are compassionate, listening people of integrity.

Integrity in the Lives of the Wisdom People

What of the lives of the wisdom people themselves? If integrity is the *sine qua non* of Christian leaders, then these people are such leaders. They clearly understand the value of integrity, they act upon it, they experience tension because of it, and they reflect on their experiences to assure that they meet their own high standards. Reviewing some examples from their lives may be helpful to church leaders as they look at their own behaviors.

The very first interview we conducted—with Pat, a nutritionist and former university professor—set the theme for those that followed. Her quote which begins this chapter was repeated almost verbatim by most of the people we interviewed. Her story is painful, revealing how high the price for truth may be. Along with some other people, Pat observed practices they all realized were both unjust and detrimental to the students. Like the others, she could have remained silent, "played along," until after her tenure review was completed, but she elected to act when the inappropriate behavior occurred, not deferring because of personal concern. The result was denial of tenure. Others whom we interviewed had similar stories about loss of pay, of promotion, or even loss of job because of personal stands which they took. Why did they do it? Pat's words probably capture it best:

> I feel I am out of a job because of my values. I've asked myself many times after not getting tenure, "Would I still do that, knowing what it's cost me?" The answer is, "Of course, because I would have had to pay a much higher price if I had walked away from my values." It would have eaten at me if I had not had the courage to stand up for my convictions.

I believed that this was the right thing to do, to
confront him rather than to run behind his back and
not give him an opportunity to redress that. That
would be totally unfair. Secondly, I believe that I was
in a position to be a conduit to communicate the
grievance. As a faculty person I could have taken the
easy way out and said, "Look, I don't have tenure, I
don't want to do this." But I had to do what I believed
in.

Pat not only acted with integrity when addressing the problem,
she also dealt with the issue of the relationship, clearly defining the
issues and giving the chairperson the opportunity to redress the
wrong. Pat typifies what we discovered almost inevitably with each
of the interviewees. They are compelled to do the right thing, compelled in the same way St. Paul was compelled to preach the gospel:

Preaching the gospel gives me nothing to boast of, for
I am under compulsion and I should be in trouble if
I failed to do it! (1 Corinthians 9:16)

Regrettably, the words compelled and compulsion are most often
associated with their pathological meaning—an irresistible impulse
to perform an irrational act. As evidenced by Paul, compulsion is
also a powerful, profound, scriptural concept. It is not a lack of
freedom, but a strong internal conviction which drives a person to
action.

Values only have meaning when tested in the laboratory of life.
Pat's values outweigh her concern for security. She comments:

Integrity means that you are just, that you are responsible, that you have values which you follow through
on, and that you are willing to make sacrifices for. I
must be willing to put my values on the line and pay
the price. These sorts of things can be very, very
costly. This is integrity. This is fighting for your
values.

Joy echoed these same sentiments. When asked what would
happen if she didn't take actions consistent with her values, her
response was simple, "I don't think I could live with myself."

Scott, who makes great personal sacrifices to continue in his
profession, often finds himself in conflict with the values of the very
society he serves. He expands on the meaning of integrity, carrying

it beyond honesty and justice to embrace a full understanding of self in relation to others:

> The value is *integrity*. There is something at the core of the thing that is solid and that radiates out. By integrity I don't mean just being honest and all. I mean being who you really are. It's got the implication of being who you are at all levels, to communicate truth and be effective, without being a phony.

The early and consistent message which Robert received from his parents was: "If you say you're going to do something, you best do it and do it right." That simple advice is the measure against which he judges his behavior. He is a successful lawyer—a self-described "prominent lawyer ...a rain-maker"—who attracts many new clients to his firm. He attributes this success to his commitment to be "absolutely honest." But that does not insulate him from ongoing tension as he works to uncover the truth. His dedication may bump against the interests of some clients. Or he may be criticized by others in his profession which has members for whom, he suggests, integrity is not a hallmark. Invited to talk about his approach, he cites situations which test his compulsion to be a person of integrity. For example, he speaks of providing opposing counsel with documents which may undercut his case. His motivation is not only that legal ethics expect it, it is the right thing to do. He describes his over-arching goal as the discovery of truth, and he is committed to doing everything that will make that discovery successful, ultimately leading to justice.

For the wisdom people, integrity is not the result of just talking about what is right, but *doing* what is right. They realize that they themselves reveal integrity in both their public and private lives. They realize that if they are to persuade, to convince, to lead others to a different way of living, they must have the courage to model the appropriate behaviors. Like Scott, they realize that integrity involves the full implications of "being who you are at all levels."

The Cost of Integrity

Integrity can take its toll, and so it would appear that those interviewed are potential candidates for stress and burnout. They commit themselves in an almost tenacious way to faithfully living the values they hold. Striving to maintain such lofty ideals is a herculean task indeed.

While the wisdom people talk about tension, they seem to be relatively free from stress. We believe it is their self-reflection and clear understanding of their values that give them personal assurance and strength. They appear to view tension between themselves and others in a positive way, as a signal that they may be moving toward conflict and as a warning that they should be especially sensitive to their beliefs and values. It is this creative use of tension that appears to shield them from the debilitating impact of stress. Where they are more likely to run into difficulty is not living up to the high standards they establish for themselves. Stress, therefore, results not so such from failing to meet others' expectations as it does from failing to act consistently with their own values.

Robert, whom we quoted earlier in connection with his pursuit of truth under the law, assures us that being driven by integrity is not without inherent tension:

> I find stress almost every day of my law practice, honestly responding to what is best for the client, what's fair, and playing by the rules, that we in the profession supposedly agree to use and are so frequently violated. I can sense that people know, clients know, that I am going to be honest even though in a given, tight, tight situation they almost might wish I weren't.

But there is a brighter side as well. Ultimately, the fruit of integrity is peace, an internal peace that rises within the individual, that flows from knowing one has done the right thing. Over and over we spoke with people who experience tension and pressure but who are truly at peace with themselves. They are recipients of the promise of the scriptures:

> Live according to what you have learned and accepted, what you have heard me say and seen me do. Then will the God of peace be with you (Philippians 4:9).

The internal peace experienced by people of integrity is described by Hillman who reports that some of his legislative colleagues have advised him that if he continues to speak in favor of controversial and unpopular issues, he will jeopardize his political career. But his conviction is that he must speak out. His personal goal is to be true to his own conscience and beliefs, regardless of the consequences.

> There are two things that are certain: there's life after death and there's life after politics.... There's no decision to make when it comes to our Christian values. If something conflicts with those, that's it. I sleep well at night. If you sat here [on the floor of the assembly, where the interview was being conducted], worried about making political decisions, you would never accomplish much at all. Concentrate on doing what is right: doing the right thing.

In terms of conflict, the cost of integrity can be high, but peace is never without cost. Arthur observes:

> I'm becoming increasingly convinced that if you are really going to try to live your life in the model of Christ, you are going to be called on sometime to stand up for those values. You may have to stand up against people that you really love and cherish and respect, and it will bring you into conflict with them. Ultimately, you have to stand up and be counted. You have to be true to yourself. This is part and parcel of what it is to live.

People willing to stand up for their convictions in spite of conflict, condemnation, and criticism may ultimately discover they have earned admiration and respect from others, though this was not their primary motivation. This was the experience for Angel who, as an educational researcher and lobbyist, had been fighting for the rights of minorities for decades. He had suffered the loss of things most dear to him and had invited the scorn of many. However, he also knew he had earned people's respect for his willingness to continue steadfastly on his mission:

> Even some people that disagree with my philosophy or the things that I do respect the integrity with which I do those things—so that even people who do not share my beliefs are sometimes very supportive. It's like saying, "I don't agree with your position, but I respect the way in which you stand up for your position."

The Need for Courage

An underlying theme in the examples we have cited is that courage is a necessary support for integrity because of the high price it may exact. This calls to mind the interview we had with Grace who impressed us with the courage she displayed by confronting hospital administrators and board members, challenging them with issues which threatened their own financial interests. She serves as a voice of conscience, pricking their sense of social consciousness so they might make decisions favoring the needs of employees at the low end of the economic scale. Her description of how she operates is simple, but unequivocal:

> I will stand up for the rights of others. I will speak out even if that position is not a popular position and it doesn't matter whom I challenge. We need to think about the human value, not just treat people as a depreciated piece of equipment.

In all of this, we are not suggesting that decision-making and action are easier for the wisdom people than they are for others. The consequences they experience are no lighter to bear. Dealing with conflict, loss of job, and being socially or professionally scorned are no less painful because one is principled. But the positive aspect is that the strength which enables these people to be strongly principled also appears to sustain them through negative consequences. Further, we believe that the peace they experience is grounded in their deep faith life.

Trying to Be Christ-Like

Perhaps the most significant stress-producing issue identified by a number of people was how to become more Christ-like in the circumstances of their daily lives. In a situation described earlier, we heard Grace tell of challenging her hospital's leadership. Interestingly, her focus was not on the stress she felt in making the challenge. Rather, it was on her fear of failing to live up to her principles.

> The stress was not the amount of money, but my fear of failing to be there as a witness of Christ. I had to pray and say, "Lord, please hold my hand tighter than you ever have during this process, because it's not easy."

Caroline echoes similar sentiments about her need to be Christ-like.

> Another tension for me is when I feel I have hold of the truth in a situation. I am a person who reacts rather than responds, and I have to fight that all the time because then I come off something much less than Christ-like.

She tells how her impulsiveness can negate the witness she is trying to give, recognizing her negative side and admitting that when she does not pause and pray, "I give counter-witness. [Then I] can really louse things up."

Robert describes the stress he experiences attempting to live his Christian values faithfully as an attorney. He believes that he has a responsibility to be counter-cultural in a profession that he says does not always encourage or act on Christian values.

> I think to be an honest, up-front lawyer is stressful because the system seems to suggest that it is a lot easier to cut all the corners you can and avoid problems by cutting those corners in an unfair way.

The pervasiveness of conflict between one's integrity and forces in the marketplace is further revealed by the situation Jack describes. He had an opportunity to direct a movie early in his professional career. "It had to do with a group of young people who had no values at all." He weighed the personal and professional advantages of the offer. It would quickly establish his reputation. But his commitment to be honest to himself and his values was stronger. While he might have rationalized the situation, trying to convince himself that he could move on to different films in the future, he realized that he would not be able to face his own children because of what he was attempting to communicate to them. To this day, his values are his guide. His strategy is to select material consistent with his values and not adjust his values to the material. This approach carries negative financial and professional implications, but it produces a far more valuable result: peace of mind.

The Pressure of Ethical Decision-Making

While all working people are challenged by their decision-making responsibilities, those who serve as managers and executives obviously make decisions which have broader scope and typically impact large numbers of people. While they may make decisions more frequently than others—indeed, their roles are primarily to make decisions—responsible executives have a heightened awareness of the ethical issues they face. As Mark, an executive in a firm with hundreds of employees comments:

> It *is* hard. I don't think there is any way to get around it, to be successful and to really work at doing the right things. To make it seem an easier path would be absurd and a lie. Sometimes you get tired.

People in such roles are realists who know that every decision they make has consequences which effect the lives of many. They can not simply be "nice guys", cavalierly making only those decisions which will reinforce that kind of image. They have to run financially successful enterprises which will generate enough income to provide employment to others. The result is that not only is integrity operative, compassion is also a strong motivation for effective leaders.

The decisions leaders make are rarely simple; each is fraught with multiple consequences. Joy discusses her inner personal conflict. On the one hand her natural instinct is to share generously the profits from her business with her employees. On the other is her need to run a successful enterprise which will continue to be profitable and provide employment to the hundreds on her payroll. She models the struggles experienced by a number of people we interviewed: the struggle to wed their commitment to being good Christians with their need to run a profitable business.

> It's very hard to be in a small business and be Christian. There is many a time when I had people working for me whom I had to let go. I did not want to on a personal level, but I had to in order to get the business to flourish. It's very hard to be a Christian, to be a good Christian and to be a business person. If I didn't have that need to be fair with people, I would probably be more successful than I am. It's almost impossible to be a good Christian, treating people like you would want to be treated, and to be good in business.

Joy's struggle to be "fair" is really a struggle to define what integrity means in her business life. How does she satisfy her need to be generous with her desire to be professionally successful? That is her ethical challenge.

It is shared by many of the wisdom people who grapple with questions related to the responsibilities which flow from being successful. Randy asked:

> My concerns have always been how do you justify being successful? How do you justify having money? How do you justify having all the things in life that so many other people don't have? What are your responsibilities to other people? What are your responsibilities to share what you have with other people? That has always been a very difficult thing for me to balance in my life...We have tried to make a good life for our employees.

Commitment to values carries a price—the struggle to know whether one is truly living a life of integrity. The wisdom people live that struggle daily as they explore what it means to be a Christian.

Implications for Leaders

The demand for integrity on the part of church leaders is the strongest recommendation to come from the wisdom people. Assuring congruity between what one says and what one does is paramount to authentic and effective leaders. The individual may possess other leadership skills, but without integrity, they will do little to encourage people to participate.

Whether we speak of integrity or of other values, the Christian leader's role is helping people understand how Jesus' message informs all aspects of their lives. This is especially true for those in the workplace where the accelerated pace of contemporary life and general confusion concerning values appear to heighten tension and stress. Most of those we interviewed commented on the benefit that flowed from the interview itself because it challenged them to define their values more explicitly. Indeed, subsequent contacts with them revealed that the interview had initiated a process of exploration, encouraging them to talk with a friend or spouse about their values. What they are drawn to is *dialogue about* values, having the experience of examining what is most personally theirs with someone whom they can trust and from whom they can learn.

Often, the mechanisms used within the church to deal with values are homiletic and prescriptive. A single viewpoint is presented—one made general enough to apply to a diversified audience. The foundational principles derived from scripture and tradition are important and must be taught, but the need is for greater emphasis on applications. As we found in our work, individuals feel the need to talk about their values, to grasp how they apply in the daily circumstances of life, and to understand how they evolve and are shaped by the environments in which people live and work.

The leader's role, as we see it, is threefold. He or she needs:

- to model Christian values, especially integrity, for the community and to be courageous in the face of public and personal criticism;
- to help people define and reflect on their values so that they understand what drives their decisions and behaviors;
- to support people as they struggle with challenges to their values, particularly those facing them in the workplace.

Reflection Questions

1. When have I not lived up to my own standards of integrity? In what way was that a learning opportunity for me?

2. In what specific ways do I need to grow as a person of integrity?

3. What is the greatest sacrifice I have made to be true to my value of integrity?

4. How can I use my position of leadership to challenge and motivate others to grow as people of integrity?

5. Does my church/group provide a safe environment for people to deal with the tension and stress they experience because of the values they profess?

6. What causes stress for me?

12

Generativity:
The Mature, Relational Leader

> I think it's an attitude of being centered on others rather
> than self.
>
> Frat

When conducting workshops on ministry, we sometimes invite participants to recall an experience when they felt ministered to. We then ask them to relive that event and to reflect on three specific aspects: what was occurring in their lives at the time; who did the ministering, and what specifically did those ministers do. As people talk about what came to mind, they almost invariably recall ministry in the context of relationship. Clearly, ministry is not simply being the recipient of another's largesse. It is experiencing a sense of being a valued person by the one ministering. What differentiates true ministry is that it introduces the aspect of relationship, and relationship brings a transforming quality to the act. It follows, therefore, that the greater the capacity for relationship, the more effective the minister will be.

Because church leadership is intimately bound up with ministry, it is our contention that people are only effective leaders when they attend to their personal development, enhance their relational skills, and focus their attention on others. This is the stage of being generative; it is the point at which one's primary focus is not on self but on people and their needs.

Such concern for others is a dominant characteristic of the wisdom people. As we discussed in the last chapter, they are, first of all, people of integrity concerned with doing the right thing. Secondly, they are generative people committed to using their gifts in service to others.

Generative people are characterized by their empathetic attitudes, concerns, and behaviors. They are other-centered, compassionate, Christ-like people, tending to place their own needs second to those of others. Their focus is external and people-oriented, not narcissistic, self-centered, or preoccupied with things rather than people. Their elemental concern is, "What gifts has God given me, and how can I use them for the good of others?" In religious or theological terms, generative people are those having a ministerial or mission orientation toward life.

Recommendations Concerning Generativity

The wisdom people offered two major recommendations for Christian leaders regarding generativity:

- While all Christians are called to be generative, there is compelling need for the leader to be generative so as to demonstrate appropriate behaviors for the group.
- Leaders need to develop models and programs to help all members of the congregation become more generative.

The wisdom people comment on the rich and unexpected dividends which accrue to leaders and congregations which emphasize generativity. They draw on their experience in business to support their views. While being compassionate and generative may be viewed as suspect in the workplace, many of those interviewed commented on both the altruistic and pragmatic aspects. Generative behaviors are often present in the workplace, helping to build relationships and assure people that they are valued. It is in this way that the work environment can be transformed into one which is more humane. Generative behaviors also help to create greater commitment to the organization; employees having more positive attitudes ultimately reap benefits for the business itself.

Effective Christian Leaders Develop Their Capacity for Generativity

Becoming a generative leader requires that one commits to grow personally. This takes more than a simple act of the will. It takes dogged determination and effort. Generativity, in the view of Erik Erikson, is a later stage in the psycho-sexual development and maturation of individuals, and demands a major investment of personal effort. In Erikson's model, generativity is the culmination of the individual's having effectively achieved to some degree the tasks of earlier development stages. It presumes that a person has learned to trust, to function independently, to risk and initiate new behavior, to work effectively with others, to attain a sense of personal identity, and to develop the capacity for intimacy. Only when these earlier tasks have been developed to a reasonable level does a person possess the capacity to be generative: to move from being self-centered to being other-centered. At this stage, the individual's energy is primarily directed toward using his or her God-given gifts to make the world a better place.

Generativity is both an attitude and a behavior. Generative people view others with a positive bias, valuing the uniqueness and goodness of those they encounter. Their behavior flows from and is consistent with this belief: generative individuals treat others with dignity and respect. These are the same attitudes and behaviors needed by effective Christian leaders.

While Christian leaders may be generative because of the work they have done on their own self-development, they also have an obligation to foster development of their people in terms of generativity.

The belief of most Christian churches is that baptism, incorporation into membership in a faith community, brings with it the responsibility to be involved in ministry and service—that is, to be generative. A primary role for all Christian leaders, therefore, is to discern ways to help all members be other-centered, ministering individuals.

Qualities of Generative People

As with all Christian virtues, there is no simple way to capture all that generativity embraces. It is revealed in myriad ways, depending on the personality, abilities, and disposition of the individual. To help Christian leaders think through how they might develop their own generative nature and foster its growth in others, we provide a descriptive definition, using behaviors we observed in the wisdom people. Generative Christians:

- emphasize compassion, concern, care, and love in their relationship with others. They regard the compassionate response not as a burden but as a blessing, describing their sense of being animated and filled with life when they go out of themselves to minister to others;

- focus on service to others' needs without apparent regard for their own;
- value being present to others, particularly through listening not only to the words, but to the metacommunication, the feelings, and emotions which are often more indirectly expressed;
- experience a sense of personal satisfaction which they believe is more than they deserve when extending themselves to others;
- are clearly in touch with their own gifts, acknowledging God as the source and understanding the responsibility they have to use those gifts for others;
- are empowering and optimistic, believing people can grow and change, and are filled with a hope that visualizes a better future;
- try to pattern their lives intentionally after Jesus;
- possess a profound respect for each individual, describing them in positive terms based on a foundational belief in the equality of all;
- are passionately committed to fostering justice;
- effect positive changes in their work environment;
- are consistent and steadfast, rather than episodic in their generous and other-centered behavior;
- reflect a sense of joy, excitement and awe;
- have an almost innate sensitivity to suffering, complemented by a large capacity for sympathy and empathy;
- have a sense of balance while living lives characterized by an attitude of generous service.

Clearly, not everyone possesses all of these characteristics to the same degree. We found in our talks that people struggle with one behavior or another as they continue to grow. But the overall image created by these characteristics is a valid description of generative people. The questions the description might raise for Christian leaders are:

- To what extent do I mirror the description above?
- Does it describe the person I would like to become?

- What do I need to do to become such a person?
- How can I motivate others to grow toward this ideal?

A recent experience we had might help, by antithesis, to capture the essence of the generative person. We spotted a woman with a tee shirt emblazoned with, "How much can I get away with and still get to heaven?" Obviously, she was wearing it as a joke, but the sentiment struck us as exactly the kind of thing that would never occur to the generative person.

The Development of Generative People

As we reviewed the interviews to discover the sources of the values which the wisdom people had identified, we were struck by the importance of early influences which seemed to fix generativity as one of the preeminent values in their lives. There is a clear pattern that runs through the interviews. Not surprisingly, the development began very early with, typically, their parents or parent-surrogates modelling what it means to be a generative, other-centered person. As children, the wisdom people saw self-sacrifice, generosity to people outside the family, and personal involvement in extending one's self to another. As adults, they now carry that same stance of being other-directed. It is intimately linked to their sense of integrity: they are driven to do the right thing and ponder issues of honesty, justice, and equity. Generativity is the inner, less intellectual, but equally strong drive which demands a compassionate, action-oriented response to needs they see around them.

Following the pattern of earlier chapters, we turn to specific incidents and quotations from the wisdom people. These may be helpful to leaders as they reexamine their own development as a generative person. In addition, the insights provided may be helpful to the leader's role of supporting the generativity of the people they lead.

The Influence of Early Childhood Experiences on Generativity

We return, first, to the powerful influences of the family on the development of one's predisposition to generativity. Kevin, a loving, giving person now raising three young sons, tells of the influences of his Italian grandmother and mother. In his eyes, they were saintly people whose lives were focused on all but themselves. As he grew up, Kevin was a keen observer. He saw their self-sacrifice, and loving concern, and basked in their love and attention. But he became something of a "wild kid," going off to the Navy where, outside the positive influence of his family, he "really went wild." For years, he lived the chaotic life of the brash young man who always knew what *he* wanted and knew how to get it. He had little time for the old-fashioned ways of his grandmother and mother until some personal crises turned him around. He now attributes his faith and his loving attitude toward others to the example provided by those strong maternal figures. The generativity we see in Kevin today was latent for twenty years. Now, he is alive with a passion to reach others, to do for others.

Grace, whom we talked about earlier in connection with her challenges to the hospital administration, maintains a deep conviction that she is where God wants her to be, that she has a call to be there, and that she is being supported daily by her God. "I believe that I am responsible, in some way, to bring God's love to other people and to care for them." There is no question in her mind about the genesis of her values. She credits the compassion, generativity, and commitment of both her parents with influencing her present convictions. She shares how her parents made their home "and their beds" available for dispossessed people in the community. She reminisces about her father's total commitment to the people of the village where they lived and about her mother's generous concern for young women who needed special care and attention. Grace is absolutely certain that her generative nature and that of her siblings is the direct result of the influence of both her parents.

Some people, and leaders are among these, are in influential positions which they can use to help develop young people. Colman, who, as we said earlier, teaches peace-making courses in local high schools and universities, relates his philosophy about challenging young people to think in terms of being generative:

> People ask our kids, "What do you want to be when you grow up?" And that certifiably is the wrong question to be asking our children. We ought to ask them instead, "How do you want to serve society when you're ready?"
>
> Get into children's heads at an early age that we expect service from them. It's where you find your joys; it's where you find your meaning.

Arthur, as a university professor, is another who uses the power of teaching to convey the importance of a generative stance in life.

He describes how he attempts to convey this message in the class-room:

> First, they really need to make a difference in some dimension. That difference has to be to help people who can't help themselves, somebody who is disad-vantaged in one way or another. Even though they are in a business school and are learning to make a lot of money, they have to realize that making money is something you do, but that's not something that is centrally important.

At a later point in the interview Arthur summed up his own goals as an educator:

> The measure of a teacher's success is whether his or her students live their lives differently because they shared part of that life with him or her.

In the four examples cited, we have Kevin and Grace whose focus on generativity was significantly influenced by family members, by people who were themselves generative and taught by example. Neither reported having had any long discussions on the need to be other-directed; their parents simply were that way. Kevin and Grace, in effect, learned by example. In Kevin's case, what was dormant for many years had to be awakened. Colman and Arthur play different roles, leadership roles. They use intellectual argument to shape the thinking of young people. Both approaches are needed, we believe, particularly today when public discussion of values often generates more heat than light. Leaders can support parents and other adults to model generative attitudes and behaviors for the young. Leaders can also teach, providing scriptural and philosophic argument for the importance of generativity.

Attitudes of Generative People

Typically, because of their early formation, generative people develop attitudes about themselves and others which influence everything they believe and do. Possessing a strong conviction about the value and dignity of each individual prompts them to act dif-ferently from many others in the way they approach their day-to-day obligations and the use of their time. John, a senior partner in a large law firm, offers such an example. Mention lawyer, and people typically think of conflict, of right and wrong, of winner and loser. That is not John's orientation:

> If you try your case in front of a jury or a judge, somebody wins and somebody loses. I feel that, for the most part, people are probably better off if they can work out an amicable result by settling out of court. That way, maybe they both lose, but they also both win. So I usually advise my clients it's important for them to consider ways to solve their problems, as opposed to moving forward and trying to beat the other side as much as possible.

So far, this sounds practical and even-handed, pragmatic advice from an experienced attorney. But John immediately goes on to reflect on what he learned from his mother as a motivation for such an approach. Embedded in his words is serious and personal concern for people:

> Maybe it's even genetic. I think that my mother probably instilled some of that in me in trying to be a moderator or mediator. The problem, frankly, is that with out-and-out litigation, you are not trying to bring people together. You are trying to polarize them, to isolate them and destroy. It becomes a war.

The need to touch people is wonderfully told by George, a successful builder, who is constantly busy, attending to a variety of projects. But his generative nature comes through clearly as he talks about his visits to a lady in a local nursing home:

> I'll bust my back running here and there. I'll bust my rear end to get over there and have coffee with this lady, Alice, every week and bring her—she likes 7-Eleven, sixteen-ounce Diet Coke—and I'll bring a brownie to her, and I'll change my schedule all around.

In a few lines of dialogue, we see George's orientation to life. Alice undoubtedly finds her week transformed because of George's simple act of being with her—and adding the brownie to the Diet Coke she likes so much.

Francis, as a middle manager in a large corporation, has the opportunity to observe people's behaviors when they pit themselves competitively one against another. He brings another dimension to the discussion of generativity:

> When someone is solely focused on their own career instead of their co-worker, the end result hurts other people. Playing the game of advancement in corporate culture at the expense of your co-worker is a very serious problem. With this inward focus on self, there is no concept of service or greatness. Christianity has an outward or outbound focus.

Failure to be generative is ultimately destructive to the individual because absorption with self blocks the growth that comes from supporting and interacting with others.

The generative behaviors we are discussing are those exercised daily. How people personally approach others through their profession and through their incidental contacts is as important as how they deal with larger issues within the community or with specific ministries supported by the church. Such behavior flows from their valuing and respecting all people.

Generative People Value Each Person

These attitudes, valuing and respecting others, appear to be dominant characteristics of generative people. Dawne, an office manager, reflects this:

> I value each person and focus on the uniqueness of each. I find that as I deal with people, meet with people, talk with people, relate to people, I am continually amazed and excited about how different we are. I don't think we can ever forget that, and I think I am reminded of that daily. Each person that comes through the door, each person that calls on the phone, is a new experience. I value the freshness and the uniqueness of each person.

Generative people not only maintain this positive attitude toward others, they also convey it through the way in which they approach others.

Mirta, an educator involved in bilingual teacher training, explains how she attempts to transmit this attitude of respect to each of the teachers with whom she has contact. The major message she tries to communicate is: "Every person was born to be excellent."

Her conviction is that if she can adequately convey this viewpoint to the teachers, they in turn will communicate it to their students.

The basic philosophy which motivates Mark's behavior as an executive is: "We are all imbued with human dignity." He sees his role as providing an environment to enhance that dignity and encourage people to celebrate it to the fullest.

Barriers to Generativity

All of us want to be whole, life-giving, admirable people. The difficulty is that we often do not have the resolve to do the necessary hard work to achieve those laudable goals. While we have the greatest admiration for the wisdom people, we do not want to suggest that the path is any easier for them. In some ways, we believe it is really harder. Unlike the poor student who does not even know what he does not know, the wisdom people are fully aware of their shortcomings and work to eliminate them. They are highly self-critical so that the kind of tensions we discussed earlier in relation to integrity are operative also in relation to generativity.

Many of the wisdom people are successful in business, and their very success causes concern. George, as we said, has achieved a great deal in the construction business having taken an early career risk which has paid off handsomely. Yet, he is uncomfortable with his success:

> I do struggle with it. I see these other rich people, and they're religious, but really, my gut feeling is that I'm wrong. We're all wrong. And really we should get rid of it. I'm still trying to explore it with a priest friend. I've got a great deal of money. I shouldn't have that, I feel. Maybe I should just sell this or that and give that money to the poor. I don't, but I do struggle with it.

What we hear is the pain of a plain-speaking man trying to balance his personal success with his commitment to be generative. He knows that his good fortune enables him to be generous to others, to build housing for those who would be unable to afford it without help. He does not use the money for his own aggrandizement or pleasure. He drives an old car and lives in the house he had when he started his business on a shoestring. But the simple fact is that George has a great deal of money, and merely having it challenges him with the moral dilemma of which he speaks. He carries these issues into prayer, seeking to know how he should act.

The money/success theme surfaced a number of times, suggesting that this is an area where church leaders might focus more attention, helping people to sort out their personal responsibilities and options.

Another major issue which challenges generative people relates to having to fire employees, not because of poor performance but to reduce the size of an organization and thereby generate more income. Intellectually, they are convinced of the need for force reduction to maintain a viable business. Emotionally, it plays havoc with them. Sharon describes the horrendous experience she endured when forced to lay off a number of employees:

> It's terrible. I don't know how else to explain it. First of all, it was just before Christmas. What do you do? I asked the president for alternatives to firing—other ways to do it. He told me there weren't any. They had looked at all other possibilities. They had to do it, if the company was to survive. I didn't realize what an impact a job has on a person's life until this happened. You see how the floor seems to cave in on them. One woman was hysterical. She just yelled and walked out crying and screaming, "You just stripped me of everything—you stripped me of my job, you stripped me of my self-esteem. I have nothing."

The experience had a profound impact on Sharon. She describes how she and her boss explored other options, both experiencing many sleepless nights as they wrestled with what to do. Being generative complicates life; it does not make it easier.

Generative Attitudes Translate into Generative Behavior

The ultimate criterion for whether someone is generative is obviously that they reveal their commitment through action. Again and again in the interviews we gained insight into the myriad ways in which the wisdom people are other-focused.

Recently we were giving a talk to members of a Christian business alliance, one of whom worked in the hospital where Elizabeth is employed. Hearing our remarks that we were impressed by a very generative employee at the hospital, the person was able, with little further description, to identify the person as Elizabeth. Her spirit of truly being with others and focusing wholly on their needs is edifying to all who know her. She is a member of a team involved in enterostomal therapy, an extremely difficult branch of nursing. She describes her work as appealing to "people who really want the challenge of helping patients who are especially depressed and feel especially forlorn."

Elizabeth knows that she could earn a larger salary in another less demanding occupation, but she is committed to continuing what she is doing because of what she can accomplish. "I have helped people to help themselves and have been able to enhance the quality of their lives."

Fortunately, she receives feedback which reinforces her belief in the value and validity of what she is doing, recalling one patient who said to her,

> Until I met up with your team, I felt somewhat like I was a leper. I don't feel that way now because I feel that all of you are doing what you are doing because you want to—and that makes a difference.

Because people are committed to what they are doing is no insulation from their experiencing doubts and discouragement. That is part of everyone's reality. Elizabeth describes such dark time for her:

> I can remember one night when I was particularly tired and I found myself thinking, "Dear God, why didn't you send somebody else? I just don't know if I am ever going to learn all there is to know about this." Very clearly I felt that I got a message. People will allow you time to learn the technicalities, but mostly what you need to do is to love these patients. Make them feel that they are loved and cared for. I felt differently about it...the fact that I really was destined to do this. I feel that it is more than just a job, it's a commitment.

Clearly, Elizabeth represents what being generative is about. She dealt with her own anxieties and fears, prayed for guidance, and came to a realization that, given her professional abilities, it is the loving relationship which she establishes with her patients that is most important.

Others reveal similar attitudes and behaviors. Raymond, the police officer, described a traumatic incident which had a profound impact on him. He came close to being killed by someone and was fortunately spared. The incident was a turning point for him, bringing new awareness of what his life is truly about. He realized that it was to be generative: "I'm here for a sole purpose, to make it better for all the people who are out there hurting."

As mentioned earlier, the wisdom people's self-awareness allows them to see their gifts and prompts them to reflect on how they might use those gifts for the benefit of others. Pat describes how she came to awareness of her personal responsibility:

> I never thought that I had gifts or talents. I thought everybody did these things that I did: that I never had anything special. Whether they are gifts or whether they are something that everybody has, they are put there for a reason and your responsibility is to tap into them. If there is an opportunity to use your gifts, you have a responsibility to do that. They are there for everybody to use.

At another point in the interview, Pat says, "What I find growth-promoting is to give things away, to give my gifts away, so that somebody might benefit from them." Generativity is where the concept of gift and other-centeredness meet.

Peter credits his involvement with politics during the Kennedy era with helping him realize that he has a responsibility to use his gifts for others:

> Our lives are really to share, and I like to think that I approach life and particularly business by giving something back for everything I've gotten. My life has been really rich and blessed. You just can't be a taker. For many years I've just had a sense of service.

Making a good living in real estate, Peter feels an obligation to "give some of it back." He sees himself "serving others through real estate and he has, for example, provided leadership in developing a nonprofit housing corporation to develop low-income housing. He apologizes for sounding "corny" but adds, "I feel blessed, and want to make the world better than when I found it."

To leave something better than one found it is to be generative.

Conclusion

The journey to generativity is an arduous one. It involves a strong and ongoing commitment to one's personal growth, to self-examination and reflective learning, and to moving from self-concern to focus on others. Although the growth process presents ongoing challenges, the rewards enjoyed by the wisdom people speak to the significance of generativity for leaders. Personally, the wisdom people achieve a sense of fulfillment and joy in their life which can only come with being other-centered. They grow in relationship with others. Professionally, the wisdom people find themselves becoming more and more effective in carrying out the Lord's mission. They influence, touch people's lives, and reveal how God's love is operative in the daily push and pull of life. People respond to generative people. Generativity breeds generativity.

Reflection Questions

1. Am I convinced that one of my major responsibilities as a Christian leader is the development of my generativity? Do I have specific plans for achieving this?

2. What am I doing to foster the development of generativity within the group I lead? Do I have specific plans for achieving this?

3. Who are the most generative people I know? What contributed to their development? Will I engage them in dialogue to discover their path to generativity?

4. What are my basic attitudes about people? Am I optimistic or pessimistic? Affirming or critical?

5. What would my institution look like if the members were more generative individuals? What would be the impact on the larger community?

13
Compassion:
The Heart of Leadership

We need leaders who are very giving, very thoughtful,
very caring, people who live their lives for others. In a
world which says "look out for number one," we need
leaders whose concern is trying to help others.

Mimi

As we have seen, effective ministry must be relational, and
ministers are fully relational only when they are truly generative.
The quality that reveals the depth of their commitment to model their
lives on Jesus is compassion. Compassion is the quintessence of
generativity. It is more than a mindset, it is love in action. Compassion is the spontaneous, consistent, helpful response to the needs,
the pains, and the sufferings of others. Compassion flows from a
profound sense of the interconnectedness of all people as children
of God. It is central to Christian belief, it is what the second great
commandment is about, that we love our neighbor as ourselves.

When we spoke with the wisdom people about their values, the
most frequent direct response was compassion. The words they
typically used reveal its many dimensions: awareness of another's
pain, simply being present, concern, care, love, sympathy, and empathy. Compassion was the value most frequently identified as an
ideal toward which people are striving, the measure against which
they judge whether they are living their Christian beliefs.

Compassion is also intimately bound to people's commitment to
integrity, but there is a significant difference. Integrity, dealing with
congruence between what one says and what one does, is driven by
an intellectual commitment to truth. Compassion reveals how one is

generative or other-directed; it comes from the heart. A touching response to our probing people's values came from Raymond, a police officer who succinctly captures the essence of the compassionate person: "When people hurt, I hurt for them. When little girls cry, I can cry with them."

Compassion is triggered when a generative person observes pain or sees another's need. However, it goes beyond feeling what another feels and is more than simply projecting one's self intellectually into another's situation. Compassion includes these dimensions but transcends them, moving the person beyond the emotional or intellectual reaction. It moves them to action.

In the previous chapter we recounted a process we use to help people redefine ministry, asking them to reflect on their experiences of being ministered to. We have led thousands of people through the reflection. Over the years, and regardless of the geographic, ethnic, or racial background of the participants, the most frequent response is that people experienced ministry when they felt the compassion of the minister toward them. The personal spirituality of the minister is revealed in the way in which he or she approaches another. The result is the difference between performing a job and conveying to another how significant they are to the minister. Compassion becomes real where spirituality and ministry converge. As St. Teresa of Avila said, "There is no better crucible for testing prayer than compassion."

Sharon is a generative person whose compassion is revealed in an experience she had shortly before our interview. In the previous chapter we discussed the pain she experienced when forced to terminate the employment of a number of employees. However, the pain did not immobilize her. Having pursued alternative solutions to the problem, she moved beyond what the company was initially prepared to do for the discharged employees. She designed and got management acceptance of a plan to help each laid-off employee define their skills and abilities, help them plan their job search, and support them in the process of finding new employment. Her compassionate response to the situation unfolded from her basic attitude toward people:

> I would think that my values are a high respect for the individual. What's important to me on a day-to-day basis in dealing with the people at work is to really see that God dwells in each one. I just walk around the facility and chat with people to get to

know them, let them know that I am there for them. You see the goodness in them. I always try to pick out that goodness in the individual: simple things that they might do, like helping out one of the guys at work who is disabled. He walks with crutches and just to see them open the door for him and to see the sensitivity people have to those kinds of things brings me such delight. I think I bring a value of compassion. People are in pain out there. There's a lot of pain and individual struggle.

In Sharon's approach to her job and the people with whom she works, she reveals many of the attributes found in those who are compassionate. She has a positive attitude about people's basic goodness; she affirms and draws out the gifts she observes in others; she functions collaboratively, rather than in isolation; she goes far beyond what is expected of her in her role (we know from other remarks that she consults with people in her field to stay current with new ideas and developments); she brings systemic change, institutionalizing her values by effecting company personnel policies (like those governing people laid off); and she grounds her behavior in her beliefs and her relationship with God. Qualities such as these distinguish the compassionate Christian leader.

Compassion is not exercised only at selective times, as the story of Tom reveals, but can be an ongoing process in a relationship between two people. Once considered a high-potential manager who would likely become an officer of the corporation, Tom went through a painful reassessment of his life after learning that that bright future was no longer considered within his reach. Occurring at mid-life, it triggered an introspective phase in which Tom worked at learning who he truly was and where he was going to invest the rest of his life. Enjoying his work and being respected within the company, he did not make a job change. More importantly, he recognized that he could make a difference in the lives of others. His compassion as a businessman is focused largely on helping others to succeed. He spoke in particular of a young woman on his staff whom he had been mentoring, patiently trying to have her see her shortcomings and supporting her efforts to change. She was not an easy person to work with, but his compassion told him that she was the person who most needed his help. When we spoke, he was beginning to see change occurring. His patient compassion was starting to bear fruit.

As a highly competent surgeon in a specialized field, Frat is quick to point out that compassion in itself is not a replacement for competence. He suggests that being compassionate, essential for Christian leadership, does not negate responsibility to develop skills and be proficient at one's occupation. Christian leaders cannot be dilettantes; they must combine compassion with competence.

> The two parts of medicine are competence and compassion. If you are going to be a physician, you've got to be a good doctor. It doesn't matter how compassionate you are if you are a quack, a fraud. And so I had to have good training. I had to be convinced in my own mind that I was practicing good medicine. That was driving me toward excellence. At the same time, I realized that, in many situations, I was dealing with families in chaos, patients in chaos, nurses in chaos over things that you can't change. Life is not always fair, and it's not often easy, but somebody has to be there to hold things together. It seemed like more and more it was me...I just seemed drawn to that.

Hanging on the wall of his office is a plague given to Frat by his staff, extolling his contributions to the clinic. When asked how he would want his staff or patients to remember him, he responded without hesitation, "I would hope they would describe me as a caring person." His goal, to be remembered as a caring person, a compassionate person, is an ideal goal for all Christian leaders. If people were to capture my life story with one quality, what would I want that to be?

Frat comments on a number of additional qualities which compassionate people value: selflessness, love, concern, sharing of pain and joy, support, forgiving and requesting forgiveness.

> What made me feel most alive, was to give myself away. I suddenly realized the key to what those patients needed: they needed somebody to love them. The great gift of life is to share what you have with others, to give yourself away. I have to be concerned about the people that I am with—staff, patients, family—concerned in terms of being willing to share the burdens of bad breaks, being willing to share the joys (if they have joys), being with them,

supporting them, being willing to forgive them when they hurt me…being willing to be forgiven, if I have offended them.

Compassion Is the Heart of Christian Leadership

Church leaders are in a unique position to influence both individuals and society to a degree that few others can. But as we discussed earlier, their influence will be in direct proportion to how their lives reveal what they believe and publicly proclaim. People will listen and follow them if what they do witnesses the qualities we see in Jesus. Perhaps his life is best summed up in the gospel of St. Matthew where it is reported that when Jesus looked upon the crowds, he had compassion on them. As the ultimate model for all Christian leaders, Jesus was primarily a person of compassion. The gospels are replete with stories of his being moved to action by his compassion.

The work of religious leaders provides them opportunities to involve themselves in others' lives at times when people are most susceptible to being influenced, principally at occasions of extreme joy and sadness. It is then that a compassionate response can make a major difference in people's lives and have significant ongoing impact.

Mimi, quoted at the beginning of this chapter, makes a plea for compassionate leaders, a plea that emanates from personal experience. When we asked what she would like to say to the church, Mimi was simple and direct. Although she chose to direct her response to a particular minister whom she encountered, her remarks are relevant to all engaged in ministry.

> I'd ask the priest who married us why someone getting married wouldn't be special to him. I believe that ministers live their lives to nurture people. When I was getting married, the priest marrying us only saw it as a problem for him. Instead, he should have seen it as a special moment, an opportunity to do something special. We need to emphasize that with ministers. Celebrations like baptisms and marriages are the most important days in the lives of the people who are celebrating them. It should be made very special and not just seen as a ceremony that they do over and over. They shouldn't take the attitude of

"hurry up and get this one over and let's get the next one in." They need to talk to the family and make it personal.

Mimi's insight into the essence of what constitutes pastoral concern and ministry is both accurate and challenging. The lack of personal warmth and compassion which she perceived — in her case, sharing someone's joy—is similar to the experience of others whom we interviewed. Blunders such as a celebrant's having to pause and consult a card to recall the name of the deceased for whom he was celebrating a funeral convey to those present a mechanical and indifferent approach to ministry. The message appears to be that the pain suffered is somehow anonymous. The ultimate result is that people come away questioning the value and meaning of the liturgical service.

While Mimi speaks of marriage as that special time when a church leader can positively influence the couple with a message they will carry through their lives, the celebration has a community dimension. It is a vehicle for helping those attending to recommit to their marriage vows, to teach those not yet married what the sacrament is about, and, in subtle ways, to help those who have experienced pain through marriage to achieve some peace. Joy speaks to this last point from the difficult perspective of her own divorce. She hungers to encounter religious leaders who will reach out to her with a loving, compassionate hand:

> I was divorced, and once you are divorced, you're no longer in the Catholic Church. I feel like I'm not accepted anymore. I feel like an orphan, like I was kicked out of the Church even though I still go to Mass.

Joy speaks painfully of her need to belong and how she went from church to church seeking but not finding what she wanted.

> I didn't feel like I belonged there. You just feel you don't belong anywhere once that happens. You're just kind of lost. This is a very emotional subject with me. I think you get to the age when you just live with it. I go to church regularly now. The good Lord's the only one that really can judge me; nobody else can.

What she experiences is judgment and condemnation while what she really needs is a compassionate response. Her peace of mind comes not from religious leaders but from her wrestling with her conscience and realizing that it is her personal relationship with God that is the source of her strength. What makes Joy's relation with church leaders more difficult is that she herself has an overpowering drive to be compassionate, fair, and just with those who are in her employ. Her approach edifies people who encounter her, observing the good she does for so many.

The woman who nominated Joy describes her as a generous, compassionate person, a competent businesswoman of utter integrity who implements programs which are consistent with her beliefs. The nominator told how Joy provides wigs for poor women who have had chemotherapy treatments and lost their hair. They suffer embarrassment because they cannot afford wigs. The friend also recounted how Joy even sends employees to the homes of women who are undergoing chemotherapy to provide them with hair care so they can retain a semblance of self-esteem.

While Mimi and Joy offer recommendations based on their personal experiences, others reflect on a related issue, adding a different perspective. They comment on the lack of compassion extended to those rejected by society, those who should be a major concern of church leaders. Jack commented on the fact that many of his peers at work are homosexual. It pains him to observe the lack of a compassionate response on the part of the church toward these people.

> I think the whole area of homosexuality is one that the church is just starting to listen to. There's a lot of people there in pain. We're not talking to these people. In fact, we're not only not talking to them, we're shunning them. These are really hurting people who need compassion and love.

Compassion extended to these people can become a powerful learning vehicle to both members of the church and to the broader community.

The wisdom people have sage advice for leaders who wish to advance the image of the church as a compassionate institution:

- Personally witness through words and actions one's compassion toward the rejected.
- As an integral part of compassion, model an attitude of acceptance and forgiveness.

- Develop the passionate dimension in one's own life so as to be more responsive to the well-being and peace of mind of others.
- Assess one's capacity for compassion through dialogue with others who can provide comment and feedback.

Only when leaders have focused on their own response to the pain of others, can they model the compassionate behavior of Jesus and thus move others to action. As Frat commented, "Most people can't get it when they are preached at, but they will get it if they are witnessed to." Frat echoes precisely the sentiments Pope Paul VI voiced in his encyclical on evangelization which was quoted at the beginning of chapter one:

> Modern man listens more willingly to witnesses than to teachers, and if he does listen to teachers, it is because they are witnesses.

Jim comments that all too often leaders model competition and hostility rather than collaboration and compassion. Territorial ownership is too common. It is counter-productive and counter-gospel, a scandal rather than Christian witness.

> We need to show a lot more love among the different parts of the church. Not only love, but forgiveness, charity, understanding. Too often what I see among the different facets of the church—priests, nuns, and laity—is competition and hard feelings. There's got to be a great healing.

Compassionate people possess the capacity to feel and be passionate. Gretchen urges, "Believe passionately." In her experience, the ministers who had the greatest influence in her life were those who developed both passion and compassion by struggling through the realities of life and honestly confronting difficult situations.

> The people who really spoke to me about living the message didn't stay within their ivory towers. They really struggled with their own beliefs. They let parishioners know they were struggling. One minister who had an influence on me was someone who was working hard enough in his own life, and he could share with you where he'd been. He lost two sons to cystic fibrosis. He constantly challenged us to

> examine what was happening, what we were strug-
> gling with in our own lives. Perhaps a theology of
> "it's all right to make a mistake and learn" would help
> those people and their message would be more real
> to folks. The ministers who [do this] have had the
> greatest influence on me.

Gretchen's remarks bring to mind a priest, who having worked in the inner city for twenty years, openly admitted that his fear of the place continues unabated to the present. When he goes away, it is difficult for him to return. "I go back at night when the harshness of life is masked by darkness." But he is committed to being there. His love and compassion for his community demands that he be there, but that in no way lessens his sense of personal vulnerability. The price he pays for being compassionate is living with fear; the depth of his compassion is revealed to others because they know that he understands the fear they experience daily in their lives.

Questions which arise from Gretchen's remarks and the priest's experience are useful for the leader examining his or her own quality of compassion. How do leaders respond to crises in their lives? Can they share their feelings about those difficult times as ways of bonding with other people who struggle with different, but similarly heavy issues? Like an alcoholic minister we know of, can they write a letter talking about their struggles and ask the community for help? Does such openness help to deepen their capacity for compassion?

Gretchen's husband Eugene, whom we also interviewed, suggests that it would prove valuable "to somehow figure out a way for church leaders to test themselves to see whether they have a consistent, compassionate nature." He is convinced that Christian ministers choose their calling because "they have a profound desire to lead people to better lives." He fears that, given the pressures experienced by many religious leaders, their initial motivation and compassionate approach are slowly worn down. Life and ministry fall into a pattern; the freshness which characterized their early work and growth fades. When ministry becomes routine, they cease to touch people's lives in a positive way.

Like many of the wisdom people, Eugene argues that compassion has to be an ongoing and integral part of the life of every minister if she or he is to truly serve in a Christ-like way. Compassion, as a value, must be nurtured to be sustained. Its greatest enemy is burnout, which results when people work so hard without relief that they fail to restore their emotional and physical reserves. Burnout and compassion are incompatible.

Compassion and Perfectionism

One of the interesting insights which emerged during the interviews was the relationship between compassion and perfectionism. A priest-psychiatrist we know once commented that many church leaders began their ministry at a time when such work seemed to attract a large number of obsessive-compulsive people. A major concern of such people is to remain faithful to predetermined criteria guiding behavior, morals, social expectations, and the like. As a result, they tend to be perfectionistic. Frequently perfectionistic people are very judgmental and exhibit very little compassion.

Sharon capsulizes what many say in less succinct ways, "I think the church likes perfect people." And "perfect" is defined in terms of "following the rules." This is a recurrent theme throughout the interviews: the emphasis of the church is too often on conformity rather than on risking to do good; on being orderly rather than stretching one's viewpoint to reveal compassion; or on determining who is "in" and who is "out" rather than challenging rules to be more inclusive. Such is not the Jesus model, as revealed in the parables. Through brief stories of everyday life, Jesus sets up situations which have predictable outcomes. Then, he introduces a surprise which disorients us somewhat in order to teach a new truth. To this day, we debate and argue the lessons embedded in these brief anecdotes, learning more and more through the dialogue. What we come to are "right answers" rather than "*the* right answer" which is the approach that the perfectionist wants to impose.

People argue for a theology, a viewpoint, and an attitude which are more congruent with the gospel message. They hope for a spirituality of failure, encased in an attitude of compassion, in contrast to a theology of perfectionism.

Mark summarizes this philosophy when he comments, "I think there ought to be a theology of accepting mistakes, picking yourself up and moving ahead." His vision for a more effective church would begin with each minister's adopting a basic conviction about the universal call of everyone to holiness and ministry. It would also embrace an understanding of the human condition: there would be no presumption that any one, including ministers themselves, can fulfill that call perfectly.

> If they could be content living as best they can and
> recognize that there will be a lot of falls and failings
> along the way, as there is in anybody's work, that
> would do wondrous things for the effectiveness of
> the church in the world.

Gretchen, who demonstrates a rare gift for theological reflection, shares her dream.

> I wish that the message of grace were more frequently
> delivered. We are imperfect beings, [but] if we can
> understand that we are loved and valued and ac-
> cepted and forgiven in the context of our religion, I
> think that enables people to go on. It allows you to
> rise above the mistakes, to try again, to look for
> another way and not to lose value as an individual. I
> think that is a very important message both to under-
> stand for myself, but for my work with other people.
> Maybe twice a year somebody talks about grace, but
> not an awful lot about how do you deal with failing,
> how do you deal when you've disappointed yourself,
> [or how you deal when] others have disappointed
> you. That you can retain the belief that goodness is
> possible.

The recommendation heard again and again in this area is a plea for preaching and witnessing to a church and a God who are infinite-ly loving and compassionate. Jack and Kate each reflect this theme. Jack remarks:

> We need more affirmation instead of more negativity.
> I think compassion and listening are two of the major
> things we need to stress. I think we get so stuck on
> minor rules. Situations are not black and white. We
> can't be so codependent that everything has to be our
> way or no way.

Kate shares similar concerns and hopes. She asks that leaders in the church "not criticize me until you've walked a mile in my moccasins." She believes for example, they have to strive to be more cognizant, sensitive, empathic, and compassionate regarding the struggles which parents encounter every day, trying to remain faith-ful to Christian ideals. Were this to occur, they would attract people to them and significantly expand their circle of influence. Kate speaks of friends and acquaintances who believe it is useless to try to convey their daily struggles and difficulties to church leaders because they believe there would be no real understanding. In spite of this, she argues that laity should make the attempt, taking the responsibility and risk to convey their concerns to religious leaders. Hopefully, this will lead to understanding and change. If leaders do not listen, they will strengthen the view that they are out of touch, but if they respond, significant personal and community growth can occur. Compassion will have the chance to flourish.

Randy and Irene commiserate with the plight of religious leaders. "I think they do care, but I think they have a lot of rules and regulations that the church puts down that make it impossible for them." They speak with a deep sensitivity for their ministers and encourage them to both live and preach the message that "it's not the goal that is important in life; it's working toward the goal." They caution that life's realities bring "interruptions, frustrations, and disappointments" as people try to achieve ideals. If leaders realize and acknowledge this, showing patience with both others and themselves, they are more likely to achieve inner peace and become more comfortable extending a compassionate message to others.

The Pastoral Response

For the wisdom people, the antidote to perfectionism and rigidity is a pastoral approach, one that reveals sensitive understanding of another's plight and which results in a compassionate response. Peter who is deeply dedicated to the church, shares an experience from his own family:

> My daughter came to a point in her life where she was branching off, and she got a little disenchanted with theology because they were always into these kinds of nit-picking little distinctions—this, that, and the other thing. She concluded, "Well, the hell with it" and found more interesting expressions, richer than formal theological dialogue and discussions. Not that that stuff is not important, but some of the ways that it is packaged, the emphasis it is given, doesn't take you very far.

As a result of his experience within his own family, Peter would invite religious leaders to be less rigid and to develop a greater tolerance for diversity.

> Don't try to pour us all into the same mold. To follow
> Christ is not the easiest thing in the world. You should
> be happy at doing it, but realize there are going to be
> some bumps and we all have our crosses. Part of
> Christianity is carrying those crosses, but you don't
> have to focus on them all the time.

Earlier in this chapter we shared the insights of Joy who at the time of her divorce did not experience a compassionate church when she hungered to belong and to feel the loving touch of a compassionate God. Chris mentions the unique potential the church has to be a merciful, reconciling force at pivotal moments in the lives of its members. He stresses the need for the pastoral, not the judgmental response to people at the times they feel most vulnerable. "There must be a greater response to people where they are, not where they should be, not the ideal. As an example, divorced people need to be welcomed pastorally."

Dawne comments on a somewhat different situation, the welcoming back of people who are distant or even alienated from the church. She speaks from the vantage point of being a convert to her denomination and is sensitive to the difficulty of entering a congregation. She decries the undue emphasis placed "on making sure everything is in order in terms of form and ritual." Instead, she proposes that the church focus on the unique gift which the person adds to the community, "bringing in freshness and questions, experiences that we have never had before."

Church leaders are authority figures who might learn from the pastoral approach which Anthony takes. As a doctor, he too carries great authority and influence on others. His view of patients recognizes their uniqueness, their personal strengths and weaknesses, and their ability to respond to the direction he provides.

> My own view of working with my patients is to be
> very pastoral. It is not to say, "You must do this. You
> must do that, and, if you don't do this, don't come
> back." It is to try and find out where that person is,
> and to try and accept that they are doing their best,
> but that this is what they believe and are comfortable
> with, and to continue to see them and continue to
> work with them and try...to encourage them to move
> in the right direction. I would like to see more [church
> leaders] coming from less legalistic, juridical kind of

teaching and more trying to realize where people are,
trying to move them into the direction but find a way
of doing that without saying, "You must be outside
of the church until you'll accept A, B, C, and D." I
think that's one of the problems, and then the church
just loses credibility.

One of the major reasons why the church has lost its credibility
with him and some of his acquaintances is its inflexible and non-
compassionate proclamations on issues, especially those dealing
with sexual and reproductive matters. He has no problem with the
church presenting "the highest ideal" provided that is balanced with
the clear message, "We want you, we embrace you, we love you, even
if you can't sustain that ideal." It is the pastoral, the compassionate
approach which should dominate. Like Anthony, church leaders will
be more effective by encouraging change through teaching and
example, helping people understand why one approach is preferable
to another rather than simply mandating it.

Conclusion

Compassion is the critical measure for Christian leaders. Because
it is the outward expression of one's beliefs and values—being the
spontaneous translation of those beliefs and values into action—it
reveals more of the leader's character in relation to other people than
anything else. From the viewpoint of the wisdom people compassion
is key to building the church. Where it is lacking there is little motivation for people to support and follow the leader. Given the breadth of
their leadership roles, ministers must be aware that each opportunity
to be compassionate is fleeting. If the opportunity is not grasped, the
negative long-term impact on the hurting individual is deepened.

Reflection Questions

1. How do I evidence compassion in my leadership role?

2. What moves me to compassion?

3. Am I willing to show my vulnerability, to let others know that
I experience pain? Do I believe that to do so would be a weakness?

4. In what areas of my leadership role am I too perfectionistic and
judgmental?

5. Have I managed my life and ministry so that burnout is not a
barrier to compassion?

14
Joy and Hope:
The Qualities of Leadership

A leader is a dealer in hope.

Napoleon Bonaparte

Pope Paul VI makes a significant point about leadership when contrasting the characteristics of those who are successful in influencing others and of those whose efforts are doomed to failure:

> May the world...which is searching, sometimes with anguish, sometimes with hope, receive the Good News not from evangelizers who are dejected, discouraged, impatient or anxious, but from ministers whose lives glow with fervor, who have first received the joy of Christ.

Effective leaders are joyful, hope-filled people. They truly capture and internalize one of Christ's central messages, "I have come that they may have life and have it to the full" (John 10:10). Joyful and hopeful people are generative, compassionate people. They convey the vitality, the fullness of life that Christ identifies with his presence. The wisdom people counsel leaders to be people who radiate joy and hope, virtues which are so needed today in a world "which is searching."

What can be said of leaders who are joyful and hopeful? Primarily, they are people of deep and abiding faith who convey to others both the peace and the excitement that flows from their experience of God's love in their own lives. They are also realists who accept themselves and the world as imperfect, but are not discouraged or depressed by this. Rather, they maintain a sense of abiding Christian hope founded in God's ongoing grace and their own willingness to use their God-given gifts to improve the world in which they live. Their optimism is based on the promises of the word—that they and others will reveal and bring the kingdom to fruition.

They accept the reality of the past, but are not held hostage by it. Rather, they live in the present, sensitive to the needs and gifts of those with whom they come in contact. They are also future-oriented, seeing options for change. They are not locked into single, rigid answers to the complex problems facing those they lead. They counter despair by understanding the differentiated needs of others and tailoring responses accordingly. Theirs is not a "one size fits all" form of leadership.

The hope of these effective leaders comes from their belief in God, in themselves, and in others; their joy flows from appreciating God's goodness, the dignity and value of all creation, and their own personal worth. These are people who, in the face of all life's complexity and difficulty, are happy with who they are, where they are, and what they are doing. Their openness, their smiles and tears, their responsiveness to others are windows on their souls. The strength and effectiveness of their leadership is grounded in their confidence that they are in relationship with a listening, loving, and forgiving God.

The importance of joy and hope as characteristics of successful Christian leaders quickly comes into focus if we consider the reverse. Who is inspired by leaders who are morose, pessimistic, backward-looking, closed within themselves? Their message seems to be, "Come, be gloomy with me." This is hardly a rallying call like Christ's vibrant proclamation, "I come that you may have life and have it to the full."

The following comment by Mark expresses this well.

> Imbue a sense of joy in all of this. If you put a wet blanket over your teaching, whatever it might be, it's not going to work. I think that a sense of joy has got to come across in all teaching, that life is challenging and difficult, but it can be a lot of fun, and it can be very exciting. I think that's something, as I hear homilies, that's often lacking. I think that ought to be emphasized—that aspect of joy.

Mark suggests some of the things which ministers can do to bring a greater sense of joy into their lives. He urges them to experience the excitement and "fun" of stepping outside their routine, safe milieu. They might, for example, go to the workplace and engage in dialogue with business people, establishing a relationship which can be challenging to both sides. While this experience may be a bit disorienting at first, the initial confusion will fade, their curiosity will be piqued, and they will gain a heightened awareness of the world in which so many of their followers live and with that awareness a renewed sense of joy and hope.

> I recognize everybody is overburdened and has too many things to do, but sometimes moving into a little different area is fun and exciting, and that's what you can do. I think that you can't have fun at something until you face reality honestly.

A similar viewpoint was expressed by Raymond:

> Everybody wants to be happy. But we as church people don't present that. Christianity should be viewed as a way of life that brings happiness, not sadness. You listen to some of these pastors and they'll scare you to death.

Raymond is not denying the reality of pain, suffering, and sin. Rather, his emphasis is on Christianity as an overall way of life that enables people to achieve true happiness. That is what he believes should be communicated. If leaders fail to transmit a sense of joy concerning their beliefs and even intimidate people through negativity, they lose opportunities to positively influence the community.

Raymond expounds further on this.

> Church leaders need to be understanding and sensitive to the circumstances of people in the community, especially those that need help. When leaders can understand the circumstances of those persons, they can then touch them.

Eugene, speaking from his personal experience, is perhaps more critical of leaders than most of the wisdom people. His call is for a compassionate, heart-centered response to people, not a coldly analytical, joyless, intellectual approach.

> My experience with church leaders has been essentially negative. I find most of them arrogant, superior and uncaring, detached and not involved with the

business of living life with parishioners. Maybe it is the result of all the concerns about budgets and this and that activity [which] preclude them from getting involved. But life is not an abstract experience.

The people that are most effective with parishioners are those who can understand, really understand at the gut level, the problems that people bring to them. Giving some kind of intellectual advice detached from what somebody can do is, in fact, useless, maybe harmful at times.

He goes on to speak of one church leader who clearly should not have been working closely with people, whose gifts would have been better used elsewhere. Interestingly, Eugene witnessed a transformation in this person, the result of his suffering personal pain.

I've watched him over a period of time, and I think he's become a more kind, gentler, caring person because of the terrible experiences he's had in his own life. I wouldn't recommend that as a way people get to be warm and caring, but I think most are just out of touch with people's real needs. Their spiritual needs certainly need nurturing and their intellectual needs perhaps. But the intellectual message that the church has to deliver, I think for the most part, has to be delivered at a level where people can relate it to what they live everyday. I have to think of all the times that's not the case—that the person responsible for guiding a particular flock is on an ego trip and is there to impress this or that person, or satisfy his own intellectual needs. They have got to focus on the everyday needs. I listen to people talk about sermons, and the ones they talk most about are the ones that talk to their hearts, not to their heads.

As we have said, a primary requirement for becoming an effective Christian leader is to be a generative person. The path to generativity is arduous, demanding a consistent commitment to personal growth. While difficult, the rewards both personally and professionally are great. A sense of joy and hope comes with being other-centered. Professionally, modeling the life of a person who continues to grow attracts others on a similar journey. Thus, the leader who reveals as yet unattained potential is far more attractive than the person who is "done." Staying on the path to greater personal growth and maturity speaks of optimism and hope; change and transformation are possible. These are qualities which attract others. Joy and hope are contagious.

To become generative, hope-filled, and joyful requires two things of leaders: first, they must attend to their own needs and live balanced lives; second, they must allow themselves to be influenced and supported by others.

Hopeful and Joyful People Live Balanced Lives

There are some people who may appear to be generative but who, in fact, maintain an elaborate facade. They meet their own needs through what may be interpreted by others as other-centered-ness. Commonly referred to today as co-dependents, these people need to be constantly nurturing, not out of a concern for others but as a way of reducing their own anxiety and maintaining their own precarious self-esteem. For them ministry is a burdensome chore. They must do the work and also maintain the facade! Clearly, these are not people filled with either joy or hope. Their compulsion does not permit them to lead a balanced life.

Pat, who exudes life to all who encounter her, models the two-fold responsibility of concern for others and concern for self. She learned how to balance these by observing her father who was a strong influence on her life but who, unfortunately, was unable to set personal limits and died at the age of fifty-six. Pat declares:

> It's up to me to set the limits. It's not like I am a sieve. What I have tried to learn over the years is respon-sibility. I have a responsibility to use the things that I am given, and I have to set limits. What I find growth-promoting is to give things away, to give my gifts away, so that somebody might benefit from them.

Given her father's history, Pat poignantly reflects the wisdom of the truly generative person, the ability to use one's gifts for others without being self-destructive in the process.

While joy and hope radiate from her, Pat, like others we inter-viewed, did not see herself as generative. A straight-talking, practi-cally-minded person, she is painfully aware of her own failings and personal limits.

> I think that I am much too self-centered to be con-
> sidered kind. I don't think enough of others. I don't
> think in terms of kindness at all, or I don't think of
> myself as being a gentle person. I think I am much too
> picky and too little for that. I don't hesitate to say
> somebody's a jerk when I think they are a jerk. My
> mother was so kind, she wouldn't do that. She would
> always see the good in somebody. I don't have those
> qualities at all.

But the generativity which characterizes Pat's life was immediately evident when we asked what would happen if she were not a
giving person. With some passion, she replied:

> Then I would be a sponge. I wouldn't be of any value.
> I would be so self-centered that I would be of no use
> to anyone. If you are ever around anybody who is
> self-centered, they are miserable, miserable people,
> because there is nothing renewing about that. You
> become your own parasite. You're feeding off of other
> people and just devouring yourself. There is nothing
> being generated.

While becoming generative is an individual and personal transformation, its achievement is significantly advanced through a
spiritual journey supported by both relationship and community.
Unless one feels human as well as divine support, motivation will
flag; absence of dialogue and feedback will lengthen the transformation process. Those who do not experience support from others
rarely live the balanced life necessary for becoming generative,
hopeful, joyful, and life-giving people.

Effective Leaders Utilize the Support Systems Available to Them

We asked the wisdom people to identify where they receive
support to sustain their commitment to live their values. Their stories
provide valuable insights for leaders who are attempting to grow as
joyful, hopeful people and who are fostering the development of
those same qualities in others.

Their responses cluster around a few major areas. For those who
are married, the spouse was most frequently identified as the principal source of support. This was more true for men than it was for
women. Many of the men speak at great length, with emotion and

passion, of their wives and the support they extend. Women speak more often of family members and friends. Peers at work were named by both men and women. However, the mentor relationship, as discussed previously in terms of values formation, appears to be a more common male experience.

The church, either as a supportive community or in the person of an individual member or leader, was identified with less frequency than we had originally anticipated. Some of the wisdom people spoke of teachers who, within a religious context, provided critical support at specific periods of development.

Finally, people spoke of their personal reflective process itself as a source of support. The ability to step back from an incident, a problem, or a worry to reflect and pray on it was seen as an important source of support. As we discussed earlier, a distinguishing characteristic of the wisdom people is their reflective ability, so it comes as no surprise that that activity is an important form of support for them.

Sources of Support

- the spouse (especially for men)
- family members
- friends and peers, either individually or as support groups
- mentors (for men)
- the church, primarily as a supportive faith community
- the personal reflective process

The Wife as Support

Husbands almost unanimously identify their wives as their primary source of support. In fact, they do more than mention them; they come close to presenting a case for canonization as they enunciate their wives' qualities in glowing superlatives. Jack reacted spontaneously and emotionally when asked who or what was the source of his support. "I thank God that he gave me [my wife]. I believe it was a gift. I'm suddenly becoming very emotional as I think about it." Other men were similarly moved when they reflected on the significance of their wives in their lives. The phrases we heard included:

- the best thing that ever happened to me,
- innate sense of knowing what is the right thing to do,

- caring, loving, and universally beloved,
- a sense of humor,
- affirming,
- sensitive,
- insightful,
- sacrificing,
- trust and faith in me,
- supportive,
- honest.

David had spoken very positively about his wife in the course of our interview. Several weeks later, we were surprised to receive a tape from him in which he further refined his comments. Clearly, the interview had served as a catalyst, triggering further reflection, and he wanted to make sure that we understood the depth and importance of their relationship and the support which it provides to him.

> I have a wonderful wife. She's amazing. She can sense when to say the right thing at the right time. She will sense when I might be down a little bit and puts in the right amount of care and concern. She'll remind us to go out and do something else, to slow down. It's a great relationship. She is an extraordinary woman who is a wonderful model of a caring and loving person. She is truly a beautiful person in all respects, and her actions and attitudes are reflected not only in bringing joy to my life but also to members of our family and, indeed, to everyone with whom she has contact.
>
> She is a universally beloved person. She has a marvelous sense of humor which has been inherited by all of our children. She claims that when we first met I was a serious and somewhat stiff young attorney, that she has loosened me up very much over the years. Our relationship is indeed a joyful one, and it's one that is shared by all members of our family. We are really an extremely close family. That kind of relationship on a day-to-day basis really is my greatest source of support. She is always there to talk out personal problems; she is very, very affirming and constantly telling me the good things about

myself. I think all of this amounts to a rather extraordinary relationship.

Anthony talks about the stress he experienced in the early days
of his medical practice when there were few doctors available in his
neighborhood. His personal sense of responsibility could only be
met with the support of his wife; she assumed major responsibility
for raising their nine children. The exalted sense of love and admiration he has for her comes through movingly as he says:

> The very best thing that ever happened to me was the
> woman I married. We just shared an awful lot. She is
> giving all the time. She loved having the children, she
> loved running the house. She is a tremendous gift.

This concept of gift comes through repeatedly as men discuss
their wives. Not only were the wives giving when the men were
struggling to establish their careers; they continue to be a "gift" with
the support they provide today. Admittedly, many of the men we
interviewed married at a time when fewer women were working
outside the home at the same time that they were raising children.
The dynamics of mutual support are clearly different for today's
young married couples. While we cannot generalize from the small
sample of younger men we spoke with, it appears that they have a
different set of understandings with their wives. They speak more
about mutual support, helping their wives' career aspirations, and
their personal involvement with raising their children.

Robert, commenting on the complementary characteristics of his
wife and himself, expresses appreciation for the way in which she
helps him maintain humanness and balance in his life.

> My wife brings real complementarity to me. I tend to
> be more intellectual, more academically oriented. But
> she brings a breath of sensitivity that always helps
> calm me down.

He describes how, when they discuss aspects of their lives, she
introduces exceptional insight into the dialogue. She helps Robert
focus on things which are not immediately apparent to him. He
attributes much of their compatibility to their sharing a "basic sense
of values" and credits those shared values with carrying them
through the typical difficulties that occur in any relationship, marriage, or family.

Once, while conducting a workshop for deacons and their wives, we found the discussion drifted to the role of the wife. Without a moment's hesitation, one of the wives stated that their primary role is to "humanize" the deacon. There was complete agreement with this assessment among the wives, and a grudging admission on the part of the men that this was indeed true. Judging from our interviews, this is true beyond deacons. We can generalize that wives help to humanize their husbands when love and mutual respect are the foundation of the relationship.

The Husband as Support

Although the wives interviewed do not identify their husbands as frequently or as avidly, there are some women for whom their husbands are their major source of support.

Irene and Randy have just acquired their second restaurant and find that they see each other less frequently than when they had just one. Irene shares how they now have "a date night," one night a week that is sacred for a planned date. The depth of the loving relationship between them is evident.

It is also evident that mutual support is provided through the relationship. During the interview, Irene identified her values as "caring and really listening," admitting that she was not always a good listener. It was Randy, she says, who taught her how to be more attentive to people and listen better. As if the interviewer was not present, she turned to Randy to say:

> I really have to tell you that everything I am I owe to you. It goes both ways in that we are just an exceptionally good match. After thirty years, when we say that we enjoy each other's company more now than we did in our first year of marriage, it is a kind of unique image.

Gertrude, with her husband sitting next to her during the interview, declared:

> The greatest blessing ever is the husband God gave me. I prayed when I was younger that God [would] give me a good life. At one time, I was going to become a nun. When that didn't work, I prayed and asked God to give me a really good husband. And every day, one of the first things I do is thank him

because we have been married eighteen years, and everyday is a reinforcement of God's blessing in my life and in my husband. My faith has grown even stronger in the areas where I am not as strong. My husband is there to reinforce me, to strengthen me, and to help me.

The Family as Support

There are important concepts about support captured in the brief commentary from Gertrude concerning the role of her family.

When I look for a place where I invest and receive love, it's in my family. I can come here and bare my heart where I can't bare my heart there [in the workplace]. I mean if I do, I'm vulnerable there. I do it being aware of the risk I am taking. Here my vulnerability is 100% and it doesn't matter. They can tell me they love me or they don't, but ultimately they love me.

Support involves willingness to be vulnerable, to admit that one needs help, and to be open to listening. All this requires a safe environment which, for Gertrude as for most people, is not available to her in the workplace. Other wisdom people speak in similar terms about their families, the people who know them best and extend support in the context of a loving relationship.

Friends and Peers as Support

People also spoke about special individuals among a larger circle of friends to whom they turn for support. It appears that there is a distinctive character to such relationships, an understanding and empathy between the two parties which enables them to move to a level of deep sharing and listening. We are aware of such friendships, for example, in the workplace where the focus is primarily mutual support. The relationship may be triggered initially by physical proximity, but over time, the parties discover that they get together for the specific purpose of talking about what is going on in their lives. They may see relatively little of each other outside of those meetings. Their special bond is that they are comfortable with each other and have developed ways of moving to deep sharing. In our interviews, for example, men spoke of the special relationships they have had with mentors. The early "father/son" relationship is subsequently transformed into a friendship which provides mutual support to both men.

The other form of support is that provided by groups. Typically composed of friends, groups can also be made up of people who gather because they share a common viewpoint or need. In such cases, friendships grow within the group. As participants gain a sense of bonding and trust, the group becomes a place where people can be vulnerable, can describe issues they are facing or decisions they must make. They can do so without being defensive.

The groups we heard about fill a number of functions in the lives of their members, helping them to achieve a sense of joy and hope in their lives. They offer:

- support in making difficult, ethical decisions,
- aid in reducing feelings of isolation,
- an opportunity to feel the care and love of others,
- help with challenging self-defeating attitudes and behaviors,
- exploration of ways to live life fully.

Gretchen, for example, talks about being a member of a group who provided her with the support she needed for making ethical decisions in her work. The group, led by a member of her church, also helped to reinforce her basic values of integrity and justice.

> He would pose these great ethical questions, and then we would sit around and wrestle with them. It was a group of business people that met once a month, and each person took time to present an ethical problem that they had run into, where their faith ran smack up against it in their workplace.

Richard, whose work frequently puts him into highly-charged conflictual situations, affirms the support provided by a peer group which listens, gives guidance, and challenges attitudes and behaviors which are potentially destructive. He indicates that the success of the group is directly related to the fact that all members are struggling with similar issues and problems. As a result, they have an extraordinary capacity to be sympathetic, empathetic, and compassionate. The group has moved to a level of maturity which allows members to both affirm the strengths they see in each other and to challenge reactions which are counter-productive. Richard stresses that being a member constantly provides him with insights to areas where he needs to change or grow.

The benefit of his involvement in the group has been extended to his church where Richard was instrumental in organizing a men's breakfast and prayer group which explores issues that the men deal with in their occupations and their homes. The bonding of the group developed so well that the members decided they wanted to do more than have their regular discussions. They started a men's chorus to sing for residents of local convalescent homes. Richard talks about how gratifying it is for them to go beyond themselves and do something which brings joy to others. The especially interesting aspect of Richard's church group is that it serves both the needs of the individual members in a compelling way, and it also proclaims their faith message to the community, carrying hope and joy to others through song.

Some support groups are less formal. Frat talks about the sustenance he receives from a group of friends with whom he and his wife have been meeting for twenty-one years.

Sharon finds that the help she needs to live her Christian life in the marketplace comes from friends, especially friends she has acquired through involvement in ongoing education and professional organizations. She declares, "I always seem to meet people who share the same values that I have. This has been an incredible blessing to me." It is to these friends and colleagues, human resources professionals, that she turns when she experiences frustration and barriers to what she wants to accomplish. She finds them sensitive to the value of each individual and to the complexities of developing and implementing sound personnel policy.

The Church as Support

While many of the wisdom people speak of the value of the church for worship, the sacraments, education, and community-building, very few find that it provides them with the support they need to continue their commitment to live their Christian values through their work and grow as joyful, hopeful people. Chris expresses not only the lack of support he receives from the church, but also his personal ambivalence about whether the church, as presently defining its mission, is the appropriate group to provide that support.

> I don't find a whole lot of support in the church.
> There's no group of business people that the church
> gets behind to help with the development of some
> kind of peer ministry. Maybe it's something we
> should do ourselves and not wait for the institutional
> church. I think most of us feel if you're doing that
> kind of thing [being a manager], that's really not
> apostolic. The real gospel call is in those people who
> in exceptional ways respond to the needs of the poor.

Chris expresses the ambivalence he feels both toward the church and toward the value of his personal "apostolate." This becomes more evident as the interview proceeds. He suggests that the source of his ambivalence are the attitudes projected by the church of not valuing what he does in the marketplace as a viable apostolate or ministry.

Gretchen's experience is quite different and, within the group of wisdom people, somewhat unusual. She speaks enthusiastically of the support she receives from the congregation she proudly calls her own. She waxes glowingly on the role that the church, the people of God, and the faith community plays in her own development as a Christian. Her experience provides a paradigm for an ideal Christian community, offering a model leaders might use to forge their pastoral plan for developing a truly caring, apostolic, and evangelizing community, one that produces members who are filled with hope and joy.

> I've belonged to the same church community for
> twenty-six years, and that has been perhaps the most
> significant relationship in my adult life, the most
> significant, organized relationship. It truly was my
> life line. It helped my children survive, it helped me
> survive, it provided the extended family that I did not
> have here. There were people that I could model my
> life on, people I could learn from, just a marvelous
> place to be. And it is a community that is very much
> involved in being the church in the world. In fact, that
> is the charge to people: to go forth and be the church
> in the world. Mission is perceived not just in terms of
> the far off, but here in the context of your life.

Gretchen describes the congregation as one involved in assisting people to see "what it means to be a Christian in the world." This community involves itself directly and intimately in many of the issues which should be the emphasis of any Christian community: providing sanctuary for the dispossessed, assisting political refugees, and opposing structures and systems which degrade or oppress people.

> Outreach is a very, very important part of the church. It is a very caring and loving church. People really care about each other. There are very strong relationships that have gone on for years and years. It is very accepting. One of the things that struck me about it when I first started was people were trying to live their lives the way they perceive Jesus would want them to live their lives.

While the support which Gretchen receives relates to her living her values and understanding her role as a Christian woman in the world, other forms of support are also provided. She recounts the response of the congregation when economic hard times hit the area. Some of the entrepreneurial members of the congregation formed a resource group to assist those who were unemployed, including providing "start-up capital."

In summary Gretchen indicates that:

> The church is my greatest source of strength, not from the viewpoint of the sermon preached on Sunday but from the belief that there is a community of like minds that accepts us and values us.

This focus on the entire faith community—not solely on the minister—surfaces as a common theme in many interviews. Clearly it is the role of the leader to foster such a community, supporting it through all avenues: liturgical celebration, homilies, education, organizations, and involvement in the broader community.

Ultimately, the value of support is determined by whether the individual is moved to action. Because of the support she receives from her faith community, Gretchen believes she is making a difference in people's lives, attributing this to the consistency between her beliefs and her actions. As a result, she is able to communicate the joy and hope she experiences.

> I am living what I believe, and I'm not in conflict with myself. And I think it would be very difficult to have any sense of strength if I didn't. I'm consistent with

my belief system and can keep on with that. I don't
have to keep justifying it to myself.

Conclusion

The wisdom people communicate their Christian faith and values
through the joy and hope they reveal through their daily lives. Their
personal spirituality is an integration of who they are, what they do,
and how they extend themselves to others. While their lives challenge
them with problems as serious as any faced by others, they are truly
generative because they have learned to balance their personal needs
and those of others. They understand that they are sustained by the
support and encouragement others extend to them.

Effective Christian leaders are faced with a two-fold task: First,
they need to develop support systems for themselves so that they
can be sustained and refreshed in their ministry, so that they are
people of joy and hope. The wisdom people make a number of
recommendations, presented here in the brief and succinct way in
which they were expressed in the interviews, that leaders might use
as a self-evaluation tool:

- Lighten up and loosen up. Do not be so intense.
- Learn to trust the people you work with.
- Do not be frightened of people, relationships, and
  intimacy.
- Do not be afraid to grapple with people's grappling.
- Do not insulate yourself from people and their
  problems.
- Open yourself emotionally.
- Do not be afraid to expose your own anxieties, your
  own vulnerability, and your own humanity.
- Be approachable and available.
- Do not isolate yourself from the problems and condi-
  tions of the people you purport to serve.
- Exude life and energy.
- Retain your idealism and freshness.
- Project a sense of hope.
- Take risks and do things to create new life and new
  directions.
- Do not despair.
- Avoid becoming secure and lazy.

- Live among the people and allow them to change you.
- Broaden your life experience.
- Be less rigid. Open up and expand your horizons.

Secondly, leaders need to find ways to encourage and support others who will carry the message of true Christian joy and hope to the world. That is at the very heart of why they are leaders.

Reflection Questions

1. What image do I project as leader, a person of joy and hope or a person of despondency?

2. In what ways do I need to change to lead a more balanced life?

3. How can I be more supportive of those people who influence and support the wisdom people in our community?

4. Who do I allow to support me in my growth in becoming more life-filled and life-giving?

5. As I reflect on the recommendations offered by the wisdom pople in the conclusion above, which ones do I believe are addressed to me?

Epilogue

The path to leadership brings to mind the long tradition of quest literature, the most famous of which are the Arthurian legends. In the typical story, a young knight is chosen to leave the security of the castle to go on a quest. Besides his armor, he is given words of wisdom or arcane riddles as aids to help him reach his goal. The journey is uneven, sometimes through verdant valleys and over sparkling rivers, sometimes through barren landscapes, sometimes through dense and forbidding forests. There are both barriers and open gates along the way, skirmishes with unknown foes, and temptations to turn back to the comfortable and familiar.

The initial challenge is to discover the meaning of the enigmatic words spoken to the young knight as he set off. They seem of little value along the road, but slowly start to make sense as the knight encounters other people on the journey who offer him their insights and give him clues. But even with this help, the knight experiences failure and wonders how he will ever be able to accomplish his task. At this desperate stage, he invariably meets a maiden. Awestruck by her virtue and helped by her advice, he becomes reenergized, goes on fearlessly to face the dragon, and emerges victorious.

While the details of these stories vary from one to another, and while the image is primarily male, the central metaphor is fairly consistent. It carries leadership messages to both men and women. The potential leader is given a challenge. Along with the challenge is advice that he or she finds puzzling, oblique, or possibly out of touch with the apparent need. But the quest is, in fact, a search for wholeness. Through solitude and reflection, though listening and relationship with others, and through failure and recovery, the in-

213

dividual ultimately discovers his or her distinctive path to leadership. This is the approach the wisdom people have taken; it is the
approach they urge for development of leaders.

The journey to effective Christian leadership is following the
Jesus model, not slavishly imitating it, but making it the creative
force that enables the leader to be authentic and generative. All
Christians are called to such a journey, but the leader carries the
special responsibility to be a beacon of faith through words and
action, to reveal hope to a suffering world, and to show that "it is in
giving that we receive, it is in dying that we are born to eternal life."

Appendices

A. Questions Most Frequently Asked About the Research

When we have both formally and informally presented the results of our research, we have discovered that the same questions are usually raised about our findings. We thought it would be of interest to readers to share the responses to these most frequently asked questions.

How Did You Find and Select These "Wisdom People"?

People were identified in four ways. First, the two researchers identified a few people who, from their personal experience, fit the stated criteria. Second, a letter requesting nominations was sent to people throughout the United States who we believed would understand the nature of the research and the type of person being sought. A description of the project was sent to both those being asked to nominate someone and the nominees. (A copy of this is included as Appendix B.) Third, we identified people in secular and religious magazines who seemed to embody the criteria. And, fourth, as people heard about our research, they would recommend someone "who is exactly the type of person you are looking for."

What Criteria Did You Use for Selecting These People?

The criteria for selecting these people were simple. They had to be lay people, currently employed, who truly live their Christian values in the marketplace.

In describing the person we were looking for to potential nominators, we also identified what would be criteria for exclusion. First, we were not interested in interviewing anyone who was ordained, a member of a religious congregation, or a lay person working as a full-time ecclesial minister in the church. Second, they would not be considered if their primary witness was what they did in the local church congregation rather than what they did in the workplace. And third, we were not looking for those who impressed people because they "prayed" in the marketplace, unless there was also evidence that their daily actions and decisions gave witness to living the Christian values in an extraordinary way.

In selecting those to be interviewed, we attempted to look for as much diversity as possible in such areas as: sex, religion, race and ethnicity, career, and geography.

Because of the relatively small number selected to be interviewed, we had to limit our sample to a single group, Christians. To attempt to make our group too broad in the area of religious affiliation would have diluted our results to a level where they would have been virtually unusable.

How Many People Were Nominated?

Over one hundred people were nominated. From this pool of nominees we selected forty-three persons and wrote them requesting an interview. Forty-two agreed to be interviewed. Only one declined.

How Did You Conduct the Interview?

We asked for a commitment of one hour. Some of the interviews were slightly shorter and some extended to close to one and a half hours, especially if the interviewee indicated an interest to continue.

The interview was semi-structured. Initially we began with an open-ended question, inviting the interviewee to share anything which they deemed might be of importance to us. We then followed a tentative, pre-established format. An outline of the interview is included as Appendix C. The interviewer was free to digress from the format to follow the lead of the interviewee, attempting to ultimately cover all the areas included in the format. Primarily we wanted to discover what these people would recommend to church leaders. In addition we wanted to discover as much about these people as possible: their values, who and what had influenced those values, the stress experienced in living out those values, their sources of support, and whether or not they perceived what they were doing as ministry.

Each interview was audio taped. A summary of the interview was constructed from the tape and a copy of the summary, with an opportunity to make corrections was sent to the interviewee.

How Scientific is This Research?

This research is qualitative, not quantitative. We cannot quote any statistics. But we can indicate what people have said. We can indicate which responses were the most frequent and presented with the most passion and intensity.

Our findings cannot be generalized to any population. All that we can say is that the findings are true for the forty-two people we interviewed. We invite our readers to duplicate our methodology and compare our findings with the responses of the people with whom they work.

B. "Ministry in the Marketplace"—Description of the Project

We recently had the opportunity to visit a restaurant in southern Florida. In the course of introducing the owners, their pastor commented that this very popular, successful restaurant loses $100,000 every summer. When asked why, the owner commented that while business decreased during the summer, he continued to pay each of his employees a full salary. When pressed for his reason for doing so, he simply responded that they had bills to pay, and that since he was a member of a Christian community, he had a responsibility to share what he had with them. As we sat in awe of this statement, he wistfully added, that he felt badly that the restaurant took so much of his time that he didn't have any time for ministry!

This story is not unique. We have collected numerous examples of other Christian men and women, living out their baptismal commitment to ministry in the same place where they live their daily lives, the workplace. The recurring theme in so many of the vignettes we have collected is that these people are unaware of the fact that they are truly ministering when they are engaged in their careers. They have failed to realize the reality which Bishop Hubbard of Albany declared in his recent pastoral, that ministry in the world is the preeminent ministry. All other ministry exists to support people in that primary ministry.

The major problem is that many people who are truly witnessing and living their Christian vocation in the world are like the restaurant owner mentioned above, unaware of being called and gifted by God to minister where they find themselves in their workaday world.

There are, of course, those who are aware of their secular vocation as also being their Christian vocation. They are a minority who realize that their Christian vocation is in the marketplace, but feel almost no support from the institutional church. These people need to hear the stories of others like themselves. They need to have an opportunity to reflect on their experience in this worldly ministry and share the fruit of that reflection with the leaders in the institutional church.

Most of the money and energy being expended by the church in forming and training lay ministers today is completely restricted to preparing people for ministries "in the church." What is needed at this time in our history, as was so forcefully declared by our Holy Father in the document *Christi Fidelis Laici*, are ways to help the laity live out their Christian commitment more fully and explicitly in the worlds of business, labor, science, the professions, and politics.

Sociologist Thomas McMahon, in a study of religious and business concepts, reported that three-fourths of the respondents to a survey claimed their business decisions were influenced by religious values. McMahon indicated that the next step is to assist "business persons in identifying, clarifying, understanding and working out these religious concepts which become components for realizing their vocation."

Goal and Method of the Project

The goal of our study is twofold: to learn what we can from these men and women living their Christian vocation in the world, and to communicate our findings to people in key leadership positions in the Church.

We propose to gather our information through a series of interviews with people whose ministry has something of a public character—that is, it is recognized by others through intentional, committed activities which give witness to the person's beliefs (as distinguished from the private and more personal spirituality which we see in the lives of all Christians). We hope to include people from a wide variety of careers, from service personnel to CEOs.

We have designed a questionnaire which will help to identify such issues as: the origin of the values which influence people's decisions; sources of support; areas of stress in living out those values; information which will be helpful for church leadership people in responding more effectively to the needs of these people.

It is our belief that an examination of ministry in these terms will help to expand general understanding of ministry that all Christians are called to be ministers and that their call is an expression of their personal vocation: living out values in the marketplace, being Christ to others in the midst of one's work. It is not simply doing parish or similar ministerial work (though that may, incidentally, also be a part of one's faith expression); it is carrying one's faith life into the realm of life's day-to-day work and issues.

We expect that telling the stories of men and women will be inspirational to others, helping them realize the potential for spreading the gospel that exists in their own lives. We hope to be able to portray ministry as a growth experience for the individual—not merely an off-hand thing, or a by-product of professional or financial success, but a compelling force which flows directly from the very core of one's being. We expect to be able to demonstrate that ministry involves difficult choices and sacrifices, that it requires energy and support.

The major product of our work is planned as a book. The book will attempt to share what we have learned from the interviews with those in church leadership. The hoped for outcome will be religious leaders who are more effective in carrying out the mission of the Lord.

We expect that related journal articles and, possibly, video and audio tapes might be produced to carry the messages flowing from the research to larger audiences. Further, the findings from the research will serve the authors' work with religious organizations, retreat houses, seminaries, schools, parishes, dioceses, and the like, so that they might shape their programs to serve the needs of today's Christians.

C. *The Interview Format*

1. Is there anything you would like to share with us that would help to understand you better or that might be of interest to us?
2. What are the primary values which guide you as you go to work each day?
3. Who or what influenced you in developing those values?
4. Were there any specific incidents which influenced your values?
5. Where do you experience stress or tension in living out your values?
6. Where do you get your support in living out your values?

7. Would you describe what you do in your workplace as ministry?
8. If you had a chance to speak with a group of church leaders what would you like to say to them? What do they need to hear?
9. Is there anything else you would like to add?

D. A Process for Listening to the Wisdom People in Your Organization

As we have spoken about our research findings, people have asked how they might use a similar process in their parish, community, or church organization. It is in response to their requests that we offer the following. We have cast the process in terms of a parish, but the reader can make appropriate adaptation to the specific ministry setting where it will be used.

PREMISES (to keep in mind as the process is used)

1. There is a need to listen to "different voices" to determine present and future directions for any church group or organization.

2. The voices to attend to are those of the "wisdom people," those who daily live out their Christian values and vocation in the marketplace.

3. There are many wisdom people who go unnoticed and whose wisdom and insights are left untapped.

4. There are many, many Christians who hunger to find meaning in their lives, a meaning that will occur only when they realize that God is calling them to witness and minister in the place where they spend their working day.

5. Too many wisdom people live in isolation as Christians because there has been virtually little attempt to identify them and facilitate their networking with others holding similar values and dreams.

6. There is a need for the church to embrace and emphasize the belief articulated by Bishop Hubbard that "the preeminent ministry is the ministry in the world: all other ministry is in support of that ministry."

7. If the church is going to accomplish its mission of transforming the world, it will only do so when it experiences a paradigm shift which emphasizes and affirms the ministry of people in the world.

8. The data contained in this book is a valuable source for all Christian ministers. However, it will be an even more potent source

if the model used to collect it is replicated in the reader's own apostolic and ministerial milieu.

Process

The following is offered as a suggested approach:

1. Carefully define the objective that collecting information will satisfy. Determine the specific areas for which information is needed and develop a few focused questions to elicit responses.

2. Establish criteria for selecting people from whom information is to be gathered. (For example, a sample of working people whose daily lives reveal their commitment to Christian values, range of age and occupation, closely-connected with the church or "on the fringe," including those who may have left the community, etc.)

3. Using the selection criteria, have a small group (e.g., pastoral council members) gather names of people who would likely provide valuable input.

4. Communicate to the entire parish what is going on and the fact that a sample of people will be interviewed. Make clear that involvement in the study does not differentiate these people from others in the parish who might also meet the criteria.

5. Carefully approach these people (the "wisdom people") and explain the purpose, how confidentiality will be handled, who will be the interviewers, and how the information will be summarized and used.

6. Conduct the interviews, using a few people to do them all. Typically, the interviews should last from one to two hours. If people are agreeable, tape recording of interviews may make later analysis easier.

7. A summary of the findings should be prepared by either the interviewers or a few people with the gifts to listen and analyze the information. It is obviously critical that these be as objective as possible.

8. Determine the appropriate timing and the best way to make the data available to the entire parish or the group which will act upon it. The material should first be communicated to the staff and pastoral council for their reflection. Ideally, the staff and council will meet together to use the data to discern where God is calling them as a Christian community. The information should then be distributed to the parish as a whole.

9. Use the collected data for developing a dynamic pastoral plan for the parish or subgroup.

Finally, we note that too often such material, after being gathered, is relegated to collecting dust on the back shelf of the pastor's office. We recommend that the information—especially that which is difficult to hear—is data to be used as a critical part of your ongoing discernment process. We also recommend that the parish will probably benefit from the utilization of a resource person or facilitator to help in the final step of the process. Usually, an outside, objective, skilled person can help a parish to overcome its ennui, defensiveness, or resistance to making needed changes in operations and priorities.

Bibliography

The following are the books, articles, and documents quoted or referred to in this book.

Abbott, Walter M. *The Documents of Vatican II*. New York: America Press. 1966.

Baker, Joel Arthur. *Future Edge*. New York: Morrow. 1992.

Bennis, Warren and Nanus, Burt. *Leaders: The Strategies for Taking Charge*. New York: Harper Row. 1985.

Borders, Archbishop William. "You Are A Royal Priesthood," *Origins*, Vol. 18, #11, August 18, 1988.

Clark, Carol. "The Pastor As Vision-Maker: An Interview with Father William Bausch," *Today's Parish*, September 1982, pp. 12-15.

Coughlan, Peter. *The Hour of the Laity: Their Expanding Role*. Australia: E.J. Dwyer. 1989.

Dulles, Avery. "John Paul II and the New Evangelization," *America*, February 1, 1992, Vol. 166, #3, pp. 52-72.

Erikson, Erik. *Childhood and Society*. New York: W. W. Norton and Co. 1963.

Friedman, Edwin H. "Emotional Process in the Marketplace: The Family Therapist as Consultant with Work Systems," in McDaniel, Susan, Wynn, Lyman and Weber, Timothy. *Systems Consultation: A New Perspective for Families*. New York: Guilford. 1986.

Greenleaf, Robert K., *Servant Leadership: A Journey into the Nature of Legitimate Power and Greatness*. New York: Paulist Press. 1977.

Hubbard, Howard J., "We Are God's Priestly People: A Vision for the Church of Albany in the 1990's," *The Evangelist*, October 20, 1988.

Maslow, Abraham. *Toward a Psychology of Being*. Princeton, NJ: Van Nostrand. 1968.

Merton, Thomas. *Contemplative Prayer*. Garden City, NY: Image Books. 1971.

McLuhan, Marshall. *The Medium is the Massage*. New York, NY: Random House. 1967.

National Catholic Conference of Bishops. *Economic Justice for All*. 1986.

National Pastoral Life Center. *NCCB Study of Lay Ministry*, Preliminary Report. June, 1991.

O'Brien, David. "The American Laity: Memory, Meaning and Mission," *America*, Vol. 156, #9, March 7, 1987.

Pope John Paul II. *On the Permanent Validity of the Church's Missionary Mandate: Redemptoris Missio*. Washington, D.C.: U.S. Catholic Conference. 1990.

Pope Paul VI. *On Evangelization in the Modern World*. Washington, D.C.: U.S. Catholic Conference. 1976.

Peters, Thomas J. and Waterman, Robert H. Jr. *In Search of Excellence: Lessons from America's Best Run Companies*. New York: Harper and Row. 1982.

Senge, Peter. *The Fifth Discipline*. New York: Doubleday/Currency. 1990.

Sofield, Loughlan and Flese, Dawne. "Push Back the Boundaries of Holiness and Ministry," *Today's Parish*, Vol. 23:19-21, April-May, 1991

Sofield, Loughlan and Juliano, Carroll. *Collaborative Ministry: Skills and Guidelines*. Notre Dame, IN.: Ave Maria Press, 1987.

Spalding, John Lancaster. "The Mystery of Pain" in *Socialism and Labor and Other Arguments*. Chicago: 1902.

Tead, Ordway. *The Art of Leadership*. New York: McGraw Hill. 1935.

Wilkes, Paul. "The Hands That Would Shape our Souls," *The Atlantic Monthly*, December, 1990.

Yalom, Irvin. *The Theory and Practice of Group Psychotherapy*. New York. Basic Books. 1970.